TRY HIGHER

THE CALL TO EVERY COLLEGE STUDENT

TREVOR FRANCIS

HigherLife
DEVELOPMENT SERVICES

Orlando, Florida

Try Higher—The Call to Every College Student
by Trevor Francis

Published by HigherLife Development Services, Inc.
2342 Westminster Terrace
Oviedo, Florida 32765
(407) 563-4806
www.ahigherlife.com

Unless otherwise identified, Scripture quotations are from the Holy Bible, New International Version (NIV). Copyright © 1973, 1978, 1984, International Bible Society.

ISBN 13: 978-1-935245-04-9
ISBN 10: 1-9352450-4-X

Cover photo by :: afte :: | www.artfromtheeveryday.com

Cover design by Novo Studio | www.novo-studio.com

First Edition

09 10 11 12 13 — 5 4 3 2 1

Printed in the United States of America

I wish I had read Try Higher before I went to college. In fact, I wish every young person today would read it, study it, and apply the truths to their lives. It will help students avoid the common pitfalls of college and also experience tremendous success in their social, academic and spiritual lives. It's a must-read.

—Sean McDowell is a speaker, teacher,
and co-author of *Apologetics for a New Generation*

Try Higher provides significant information and practical application that engages students to find purpose in their college experience benefiting them now, in their career, and into eternity. The significance of this book is priceless and should be in the backpack of every high school graduate and college undergrad.

—Pastor Justin Williams, The Refuge of Bentonville, Arkansas

This book is clear, concise, positive and practical. I especially recommend this book for those whose faith is central and who desire to make a difference in college and throughout life."

—Dr. Rex M. Horne, Jr., President of Ouachita Baptist University

...a useful, encouraging, and inspiring guide.

—Lyna Lee Montgomery, University of Arkansas, Professor of English

I believe this book will become a compass for all aspiring young men and women who wish to become somebody in life. Many have failed because they didn't have such a tool.

—Pastor Sunday Adelaja, Senior Pastor and Founder,
Embassy of God, Kiev, Ukraine

Try Higher is a great book to guide students through the most critical time in life. It is a great way to help students think about the impact they can have throughout college that will prepare them for the future.

—Shawn Smith, Student Pastor,
First Baptist Church of Springdale, Arkansas

What a great concept for every college student to read! Trevor Francis challenges college students to go beyond just wondering "What should *I* do with my life?" and asks the better question "What does *God* want me to do with my life?"

—Dr. Joe White, President of Kanakuk Kamps

It's not a book about philosophy or theory it's a practical solution-driven handbook for every college, or college-bound, student. Trevor takes the best advice for academic success, mixes in a motivational call-to-action, and weaves solid advice for spiritual growth and leadership through every page. Like having an encouraging life-coach at your side.

—Josh Jenkins, Student Minister,
New Hope Fellowship

As a Christian and a university professor I am encouraged in Trevor's view that going to college is not something that a follower of Christ should fear will damage their faith, rather an incredible opportunity to put their faith in action and make a difference in the college or university where God has led them - very encouraging."

—Dr. Michael Reed, Professor of Mathematics,
Tennessee State University

There are very few books that speak to the struggles faced during college. Trevor has helped fill this chasm in a way that is not only practical, but also gives spiritually mature advice. In my opinion, the more students that get a hold of this and read it the better!

—Chuck Bomar (CollegeLeader.org),
author of *College Ministry 101: A guide to working with 18-25 year olds*

We have a secular university culture that hates Christianity and is pro-active in trying to destroy it in our kids. Let this book be a powerful companion to parents and youth leaders everywhere to prepare Christian kids for the war and the inspiring challenges that await them!

—Brad Stine, Comedian/Actor/Author/Christian worldview advocate

Try Higher beautifully blends practicality and spirituality for the college student. This should be required reading for every student, and recommended reading for everyone else!

—Dr. Tom Blackaby,
author of *The Family God Uses, Encounters with God Daily Bible*,
co-author *The Man God Uses, Blackaby Study Bible, Companions of Paul*,
International Director, Blackaby Ministries International,
t.blackaby@blackaby.org

*don't act thoughtlessly, but **try** to find out and do **whatever the Lord wants** you to*

(Ephesians 5:17 TLB; emphasis added)

Acknowledgments

THANKS TO MY FAMILY for being so fun and for being an inspiration with the details of your life. This book is dedicated to you. Mom and Dad, thanks for your kind hearts, sincerity, and for always modeling servant leadership. This book was first your message to me. Dennis and Jinny, thanks for being such wonderful encouragers and great examples. I can't imagine my life without the two of you. To Kenneth Francis, my Pawpaw, thank you for your excellent spirit; you're an inspiration to me and everyone you meet. Nicole, thanks for being such a great wife and for being patient with my extra energy. Thanks for being my best friend.

To Grace Bible Church—Jan & Jerry Boseman, Robert & Beverly Carter, Ken & Donna Francis, and Mike & Bernice Stolz—thank you for helping make this book a reality. To Aunt Patti and Uncle Tony, thanks for believing in us. To Lyna Lee Montgomery, thank you for taking the time to read through and edit my early manuscript. To Josh Jenkins and Justin Williams, thanks for voicing your encouragement and support at just the right time. Thanks to Dave Dawson and the Fulbright College Advising Center for helping me see the significance of the details in our educational plans and for the importance of guiding students during college. To my editor, Chris Maxwell, thanks for your encouragement and for taking my words to the next level. To Dave Welday, Marsha McCoy, and the HigherLife Team, thank you for your guidance and encouragement.

Thank you, God, for prompting my heart at just the right times in life, for showing me which steps to take and when during my journey. Your plans are perfect, and the good that you offer is incomparable to all else. Thanks for inspiring me to be my best and for helping me to share my experiences with others.

Contents

Introduction 1

Chapter 1   Your Spiritual Guide 3

Chapter 2   A Higher Education 5

Chapter 3   Purpose During College 7

Chapter 4   Opportunity 11

Chapter 5   Small Things, Big Heart 13

Chapter 6   Just Shine 15

Chapter 7   About Truth 19

Chapter 8   A Compelling Choice 27

Chapter 9   Spirit-Filled Learning 35

Chapter 10 Spiritual Motivation 41

Chapter 11 Go to the Ant 47

Chapter 12 Communicate! 53

Chapter 13 Relentless Relationship 61

Chapter 14 Isolated or Inspired? 71

Chapter 15 Higher Confidence 91

Chapter 16 Reference Point 95

Chapter 17 Four Significant Years 99

Chapter 18 Your Purpose, God's Provision 113

Chapter 19 Discover Your Destiny During College 119

Chapter 20 *try* Inspired 133

Appendices

Appendix 1:   *try* Exploring Your Major 145

Appendix 2:   *try* College with Purpose 147

Appendix 3:   *try* A College Plan...................................... 148

Appendix 4:   *try* Focused Motivation! 152

Appendix 5:   *try* 5 Reasons —College Students Succeed 154

Appendix 6:   *try* A Checklist—Presentations and Papers... 156

Appendix 7:   *try* A Checklist—Presenting My Ideas 157

Appendix 8:   *try* Money Vision.. 158

Appendix 9:   *try* Vision to Reality 160

Appendix 10: *try* 3 Learning Steps—Seeing to Living.......... 161

Appendix 11: *try* Stress Management 163

Appendix 12: *try* Relationship Peace............................... 164

Appendix 13: *try* Higher Transition 165

Appendix 14: *try* Spiritual Preparation—Five Tips.............. 166

Appendix 15: *try* College Resources 168

Endnotes..173

Introduction

try Higher

The Christian ideal has not been tried and found wanting. It has been found difficult; and left untried.

—G.K. Chesterton[1]

WHERE ARE THE SPIRITUAL leaders on college campuses? Where are college students willing to write their own script instead of accepting what campus life hands them? Where are students of clarity, initiative, and resolve?

This generation—you and the students who will experience college with you—crave a call, an invitation, a motivation, to live life at higher levels. There's an urgent call for you to live with purpose. Destinies are at stake. It's time to see the details of your life as central to finding your unique mission. It's time to hear a different perspective, to see a different story emerge from our campuses.

Many students don't consider themselves leaders. But think about it this way: if your inner person has been changed, then, by nature, you've been called to lead. I've asked deep questions to the unassuming student leaders I've met. They always suggest a spiritual approach to college, a perspective that points beyond self to the One "higher than I" for encouragement and true direction.[2] They say, "He wants us to live up to our full potential."

So, why not try college a different way? His way.

Your Spiritual Guide

TELL ME ABOUT YOUR spiritual journey," he said.

During college, my friend Tim invited me to his grandparents' house for a 4th of July cookout. I hadn't been there five minutes; his Grandpa was already inquiring into my life. Not many people ask— and few seem to care—about what you're going through in life. So I welcomed the interest. Before I knew it, the topic had turned to my spirituality.

During his years as a pastor, Tim's Grandpa had learned to ask others about their spiritual journeys. He suggested I do the same. By taking this approach, he was able to get people talking about their experiences, what they were going through, and how they were doing. He took conversation to a deeper level while infusing it with encouragement. I enjoyed the simplicity and depth of his words.

Our short conversation motivated me to evaluate my experiences as a student. I was encouraged to remember my purpose during college, to see it as a significant chapter in my spiritual journey. I remembered how unprepared I had felt for college and how that caused me to look beyond myself. I felt challenged to find purpose and motivation each semester.

Now I'll ask you those questions. How is your spiritual journey? How is college? Do you see depth in your experiences? Are you living at your best? Helping others? Growing?

The One who led you here is deeply interested in your unique college experience. He has a passion for your potential and your progress as an individual. He cares about you becoming a friend to others. He wants to use college to shape your character and to inspire you into the life of which you and your family have dreamed.

Let Him guide you during college. He can use all of your experiences—your professors, learning style, major, small decisions, advisors, campus life, commuting, and other students—to refine your integrity and help you discover your destiny.

To *try* Higher

1. See college as a spiritual journey involving the development of heart.
2. Know that you have the spiritual guide for your journey, someone to always rely on for advice and direction: "But when he, the Spirit of truth, comes, he will guide you into all truth" (John 16:13).

A *Higher* Education

W E JOTTED DOWN, IN rank order, 20 words that answered the question, "Who am I?" Our social psychology professor was having us take Kuhn's self-attitude test. If *self* was the "sum total" of who we are, as C.G. Jung suggested, I wondered how the other students would sum up their identity.[1]

Some described personal qualities: "I'm athletic, nice, good-looking." Others used social descriptions: "I'm a friend, sister, cousin." Finishing, I glanced back to the top of my paper, "child of God." A deep contentment stirred in my mind, but how did the others feel? Did they also have a central description of who they were? I was reminded that we were not all alike. Views about our core identities were different for each person who wrote. So was our understanding of reality. Similar college experiences can bring different educations.

I like to use the term "higher education" to describe college. "Postsecondary education," "university," and "community college" are descriptive, but "higher education" gets at the dimension of why we're in school. We're not just here to become more self-aware, learn more information, decide on a major, or to find a job. We have been called here to grow deep in our understanding of our relationship with the Creator. We're here to learn how to think and live higher.

We pursue education "to get a crown that will last forever" (1 Cor. 9:25). We are not motivated by the reward of getting ahead in life, gaining prestige, or simply making the grade and earning a diploma. We're running to receive a prize that will last forever. Our track is spiritual, and our stride on the road to success is unlike that of temporary crown competitors. Your attitude concerning college is different when you know the Mind behind the universe. You are a child of God; He has a higher purpose for you during college.

try Higher Thoughts

1. Think about the spiritual dimension to college: "Set your minds on things above, not on earthly things" (Colossians 3:2). Do you see the reality of His thoughts at work in your experiences, classes, and in your relationships? Do you give every thought to Him?
2. Inspire others to live higher. To do this, there should be a recognizable difference between you, His child, and those who do not know Him.
3. To go higher, first grow deep. Oak trees can only grow as tall as their support roots allow. Grow deep in your faith by allowing God to show you your purpose each day during college.

Purpose During College

ENTELECHY"...our philosophy professor said Aristotle used the word to describe the potential of an acorn. Within an acorn lies the potential of an oak tree. At full potential, the acorn is a remarkable oak.

The word stuck with me. What was my entelechy? My full potential? In my heart I knew I had potential, but I wasn't sure of a specific major or career. I did know my current purpose, though: to do my best now, to help those who were in college with me, and to leave college better than when I had come in. College, if lived fully, would provide significant opportunities for discovering my destiny.

God has a purpose for you during college, not just after graduation. Watch for His design at work while sitting in class, reading assignments, exploring your major, living in a dorm, and making friends. He has certain people that He wants you to encourage, certain people that He wants to encourage you. You are to teach and to be teachable. You are to serve others and at times to let others serve you. You are not in college by accident. You are attending your school and taking your particular courses as part of His plan for your life and for others. See the value and purpose of this experience for you.

Your campus is an ideal place to learn and practice your purpose. Even in thinking about attending college you have the chance to grow. By envisioning your future, you can develop your reasoning skills, gain a deeper understanding of your personality, clarify your values, and practice listening to God. Because college is where He has you right now, listen to Him about your purpose during the process. Know that you are to grow and to encourage others along the way.

Learn and Lead

Ancient Mesopotamia (modern Iraq) was the location of the earliest known institutions of formal learning. If you were literate in this society, you were a person of influence. Scribes trained in record keeping—a style called "cuneiform"—had influence, especially with their leaders. As agricultural society became more complex, the need for record keeping grew. As a result, the need for trained individuals increased. Today, we have the same need for trained individuals. As our society grows more complex, there is a call for effective leaders to meet our changing needs.

A place of influence can be an opportunity to help many people. Think of Daniel in the Old Testament. God used his education and integrity to place him in a position in which he could help many people. If God knows that your heart is obedient, why wouldn't He put you where your training and integrity join to help meet the greatest needs of society? It may not be your first choice, but it will be where He needs you most. When Jabez cried out, "Oh, that you would bless me and enlarge my territory," God granted his request and increased his influence (1 Chronicles 4:10).

The One who created you cares about helping you get the education you need to fulfill your unique mission in life. He has used trained individuals to transform many lives. Luke was a medical doctor. Paul was an expert in religious studies. Daniel completed a three-year program with an emphasis in literature and languages. God used their studies to develop, promote, and sharpen them for service. They added to their knowledge and sought guidance, and He promoted them to a place where they could use what they had learned.

Your campus is working to provide you with an atmosphere of freedom and structure so you can become a person of influence. Seize the opportunities before you, and watch as God teaches you about His plan for your potential. See the value in the opportunity before you. Follow Solomon's advice, and "let the wise listen and add to their learning, and let the discerning get guidance" (Proverbs 1:5).

try Purpose

1. Do you see the importance of the college process in developing you and your ability?
2. Know that your role as a student is significant. Step up to your new responsibilities and live with practical spirituality (see Proverbs).
3. See the value in conversations with other students, with staff, and with faculty.
4. Ask God to make clear your motive for being in college.

Opportunity

COLLEGE IS A CALLING. If you don't see this, then it will be hard to reach the height of your potential before and after graduation. As a student, your Lernfreiheit—*freedom to learn* (courtesy of medieval European universities)—should be fully enjoyed but never overlooked.[1] If we are unappreciative and unaware of the depths of opportunity before us now, how can we reach our best? Immense reservoirs of motivation and passion spring forth from our hearts when we realize where God's design has brought us and that He intends to lead us into victory. Listen to Rich Stearns, president of WorldVision, as he writes about his own college opportunity:

> As an alumnus myself, singing the Cornell alma mater at the end of Hannah's [his daughter] graduation ceremony took me back 43 years to 1964, when at the age of 13, I wrote to all eight Ivy League colleges requesting their catalogs. Back then, I would lie awake at night, paging through their course listings, trying to imagine what it would be like to actually attend one of the schools. You see, my father never finished the eighth grade, and my mother never completed high school. My parents were divorced, and there was no money, so the possibility of this dream coming true seemed remote. But 11 years later—through God's grace, hard work, scholarships, and loans—I had graduated from both Cornell University and the University of Pennsylvania. That tremendous opportunity allowed me to pursue my dreams and give the same opportunity to my five children[2].

For Rich Stearns, college was a dream and a privilege. His vision, hard work, and sense of destiny of pursuing an education were the impetus in his success during and after college. His college opportunity helped him to fulfill his unique calling to his family and to those in need.

In contrast to many of the world's population, you have incredible access to education. In total, 115 million children worldwide are not able to go to school.[3] If you grasp the opportunity of being a student, you will more fully pursue the unique purpose that has been placed within you. An appreciative heart is a motivated heart; the result of this kind of drive is dream realization.

Be glad for the ability to learn and the opportunity to attend college. Realize that your experiences are designed to have a significant effect beyond the present. And, your response to your current opportunities will be used to help provide others with opportunities to fulfill the plan God has for them.

try Gratitude

1. Start now by letting God know that you are thankful for your college opportunity.
2. Know that He is at work right now in your life. Think about why He has allowed you to be a student at the school you are attending. Whom are you to help? To learn from? What's the mission of the school? Your unique mission?
3. Stay balanced while making the most of every opportunity. Look into the many campus opportunities that can help you grow: research, service learning, volunteer, guest lecture, study abroad, part-time job, and conferences.
4. Choose to set your heart on things above (Colossians 3:1). Don't get distracted by what others are doing, but determine to live with integrity in the small things.

Small Things, Big Heart

J AKE, 25, RETURNED TO school after working full-time since graduating from high school. We ended up in the same introductory sociology course along with 350 other students. During the second class, our professor had us form groups of 3-4 to work on team papers. Jake happened to be sitting next to me.

After the first assignment, our other teammate dropped the course, so Jake and I were left unaided to work on the papers. Jake was anxious about his writing, and I was too, but I did my best to encourage him and to show him the strategies I had learned in my intro composition course.

As we continued in the course, I knew that I needed to be talking to God for Jake. I wanted him to experience the good in knowing God. Near the end of the semester, Jake and I were walking to our cars to leave; we both lived off campus. Before he got into his truck, he told me he had been thinking about whether or not there was a God.

He said that recently he had not been able to sleep at night (interestingly enough, his sleep deficiency started near the same time that I started praying for him). He felt that God was trying to tell him something; he just didn't know what, and he was interested in what I thought. I told Jake I knew what God was telling him. I told him that the same God who had created the universe wanted to have a relationship with Him. I explained that religion was man's search for God, but that Christianity was God reaching down to us (hence the pull he felt within). I helped Jake offer his life to the Maker of his soul in a parking lot next to the football stadium at our large research-based university.

Before the semester started, I knew I wanted to be my best and to do whatever God asked of me. I knew that my purpose in each class was to work hard on assignments, to think and grow deep, to get to know my professors, to live truth, and to just be myself. When Jake came into relationship with God, I was only doing small things: going to class, getting involved the best way I knew how with my group, talking with the professor and teaching assistants, learning how to improve my writing, sharing the things I was learning, helping others to succeed, speaking my faith when led, and praying for the person that God had placed on my heart.

I was faithful with just being a student, and God used it for good. Mother Teresa says, "We can do no great things; only small things with great love."[1] When we are faithful with being a student, growing at the school we are in, God is able to work in us to accomplish His purposes. Our purpose during college is to see His purposes abound.

Wouldn't it be satisfying to remember your college experience as being a student who recognized and seized the tremendous opportunity before you? If you choose to be like Daniel during your education and to live with integrity in all areas, even small, then watch as God uses your often perplexingly ordinary life in brilliant ways. Your purpose during college is to do small things with great love and to leave the exponential results to God.

try Small Action

1. See the details of your life as significant.
2. Help someone study or show someone a learning strategy you've picked up. Show another student how to write a good paragraph or how to work a math problem.
3. Keep some extra pencils and scantrons on hand and give them to those who forget them during a test. Do something creative for the staff at your school, something that shows them you're thankful for their help and support. Try writing a thank-you letter or bringing them some cookies.
4. Tell another student that you enjoyed his presentation, or tell a professor that you like her class.
5. Can you think of other simple but life-giving actions?

Just *Shine*

We are stars, bold, blazing, light-giving stars!
No need to shout, scream, or make a scene.
Just Shine.

—Charles Swindoll[1]

AS A COLLEGE STUDENT, when you choose to shine by listening to God's voice in the details, you allow His light to find its way into the hearts of students, staff, and professors around you. Wouldn't it be inspiring to see campuses—among the most influential of social institutions—ablaze with kindness and truth because students just decided to shine? Listen to how several students and professors influenced the life of Josh McDowell as he tells his own story in *More Than a Carpenter*. In the midst of a turbulent struggle during college to understand life and reality, he remembers:

> I suspect that few people in the universities and colleges of this country were more sincere in trying to find meaning, truth, and purpose in life than I was. I hadn't found it yet, but I didn't realize that at first. In and around the university I noticed a small group of people: eight students and two faculty members, and there was something different about their lives. They seemed to know why they believed what they believed. I like to be around people like that. I don't care if they don't agree with me. Some of my closest friends are opposed to things I believe, but I admire a man or woman with conviction. (I don't meet many, but I admire them when I meet them.) That's why I sometimes feel more at home with some radical leaders than I do with many Christians. Some of the Christians I meet are so wishy-washy that I wonder if maybe 50 percent of them are masquerading as Christians. But

the people in this small group seemed to know where they were going. That's unusual among university students.

The people I began to notice didn't just talk about love. They got involved. They seemed to be riding above the circumstances of university life. It appeared that everybody else was under a pile. One important thing I noticed was that they seemed to have a happiness, a state of mind not dependent on circumstance. They appeared to possess an inner constant source of joy. They were disgustingly happy. They had something I didn't have.

Like the average student, when somebody had something I didn't have, I wanted it. That's why they have to lock up bicycles in colleges. If education were really the answer, the university would probably be the most morally upright society in existence. But it's not. So, I decided to make friends with these intriguing people.[2]

Isn't that great? Josh's story is inspiring because it illustrates the best approach for influencing our campuses. Josh perceived the joy difference in a few college students and faculty, a divergent group willing to live above stress and above circumstances. Tired of existing in his own darkness, his own "hell" as he described it, he was drawn to the life-giving light that these spiritual leaders reflected. He even found them intriguing.

After being pulled into a close relationship with these students and professors, Josh wasn't disappointed. He didn't find himself talking to immature individuals who had no idea how to discuss faith with intellect. Instead, they challenged him to evaluate the evidence of the Creator's Son; a task he took to heart as he wrote *Evidence that Demands a Verdict*.[3] They were able to teach him that people of faith live with integrity and they have the ability to give sound reasons for their trust. They were "prepared to give an answer to everyone who asks" for the cause of their hope and joy-filled perspective (1 Peter 3:15-16).

Like the students Josh met, you have profound influence as a student in higher education. You and the students around you directly influence our world. Higher education, in many regards, is the common denominator in the equation of preparing leaders who can initiate positive change in our culture. Who will stand and face our challenges in health care? In science and engineering? Who will bring excellence to our education system? Who will bring an insightful perspective to our justice system? Who will bring integrity to business and industry? Who will use their political influence and knowledge of government to help society? Who will answer our need for spiritual leadership? Will the nearly 18 million students who are being trained in our colleges and universities answer the urgent call for leadership in these areas?[4]

Charles Malik, former President of the UN General Assembly, says "The universities...directly and indirectly, dominate the world; their influence is so pervasive and total that whatever problem afflicts them is bound to have far reaching repercussions throughout the entire fabric of Western Civilization,"[5] and Dr. J Stanley Mattson, President of the C.S. Lewis Foundation, adds, "the university serves as the center for the development and training of the entire professional class of the next generation—our teachers, professors, journalists, lawyers, jurists, politicians, business leaders, scientists, engineers, health care professionals, film and television executives and producers, not to mention pastors and prophets of every persuasion."[6]

That's why your term papers, your presentations, kindness, encouraging words, and your excellence within each course are so important. You are bringing light to others. If you take 40 classes to earn your four-year degree and there are 30 students in each class, then by the time you finish you will have been in class with 1,200 students. If you just consider the 4 students sitting around you in class (in front, on either side, and behind you), that's 160 students you will be next to in class. Add 40 professors to that number, and you are in close contact with 200 people. If you add the people you meet through work or internships, volunteer experiences, your dorm, apartment, and student organizations, the numbers dramatically increase. Higher education, with its diversity of people and ideas and its influence, is an extraordinary place to shine.

As you live your best during college, see the urgency in influencing your campus; see the need for developing your full potential. As you live with purity in your spirit, others will be inspired to look higher and to carry good with them into their careers. Be willing to let God use you to help those around you become people of integrity. Be obedient so that others can know truth and so that ceaseless good can be done in the hearts of those who influence each area and institution in society.

The sooner we get about doing the seemingly small tasks right in front of us, growing deep with the friends who are near us, the more realistic we will be and the closer we will be to bringing positive change to our college classrooms, dorms, campuses, and our communities. Profound statements, packaged in small action, have tremendous effect. If we want to answer God's call to learning and to helping others, then unquestionably "We must become the change we want to see in the world."[7] Start with the classes that you're in this semester. Through the tasks and relationships closest to you, realize this: You are changing the world.

try Joy

1. You have a relationship with God; so enter His peace, and live above your circumstances. Live with joy.
2. Be approachable and kind. Speak a word of encouragement to another student, a graduate assistant, a professor, or someone on staff at your school.
3. Learn to share truth by first living it. When God's Spirit prompts you to speak, your words will have influence because they are in agreement with your life.
4. Desire to see life and people from the Creator's perspective. Cry out, "God help me to see myself and others the way that you do."

Chapter 7

About Truth

Loving the Lord with your *mind* means understanding God's ordinances for all of creation, for the natural world, for societies, for businesses, for schools, for government, for science, for the arts...

— Chuck Colson[1]

COLONIAL INSTITUTIONS OF HIGHER learning communicated a sense of nobility in their school mottos. "'Veritas' conveyed Harvard's quest for truth, and 'Lux et veritas' (light and truth), Yale's commitment to revelation and reason."[2] These campuses were concerned with the transcendental, the spiritual, during college.

As students, we're interested in how things work and the *why* behind them. Our desire to know truth is our longing to know reality. We want to see clearly so we can improve our lives. Deeper, we want to know who we are and our place within the universe. We long to know the Maker.

Our quest for truth is our desire to know the Mind with which we once lived in perfect intimacy. Human inquiry of meaning, the result of our lost ability to see with perfect perception, can only be deeply satisfied, as Dietrich Bonhoeffer says, through spiritual means: "To understand reality is not the same as to know about outward events. It is to perceive the essential nature of things."[3] When we're in right relationship with the One who perceives perfectly, our desire and ability to see spiritual truth is restored because He is the essential life of all reality (Colossians 1:17). If you want to know reality during college, get to know the Creator and His original purpose for people, His answer to our descent, and our destiny. (See Genesis 1; Romans 3:23-24; Revelation 20-22.)

See beyond the system at work around you during college and you will see the deep need for God's ordinances. Like the colonial institutions, your motto will reflect a desire to know truth, and, out of that, a heart for helping others know reality will surface. You'll be like Brown University who "placed its hope in God with 'In Deo Speramus.'"[4]

Campus Truth

I talked with two students once who were caught signing in for each other during an Intro to College class. There were no tests for the course; their pass/fail grade was based only on attendance. When confronted about their choice, they initially responded by saying they were just trying to be good friends to each other. They had no clue of the darkness of their decision. I asked them what their employer would do if one of them had been caught clocking in for the other. The look on their faces said they were starting to understand. I explained that because the course was based solely on attendance, they had essentially shown up and taken the test for the other. When explained in those terms, it didn't take long for them to come into the reality of their choice. By the end of our conversation, they were able call their decision what it was—cheating. They could call it nothing else.

Truth is defended constantly on college campuses and not just in classroom discussions or in debates among friends. Have you ever heard the phrase, "You can't legislate morality"? It is impossible to create campus policy which ensures that all students have an honest motive. Instead, your Dean of Students can enforce policy that says you cannot act on a dishonest motive by plagiarizing a term paper. You can't be given an honest heart by your campus administrators and professors, but they can penalize you when you are caught stealing ideas or signing in for someone else. They cannot keep students from allowing lustful thoughts to consume their minds, but they can banish them from campus and turn them over to the local authorities for raping another student.

No one can be forced to be an honest, moral person, but he can be punished for acting on a dishonest, immoral motive. Right standards cannot change our nature, but we can see the reflection of our inner person and our immoral motives through their mirror. While we cannot force a moral heart, we can insist on moral behavior and boundaries by creating sound campus policies. So, in a sense, truth and morality are defended every week by your judicial board, by campus police, by syllabi that insist on honest course work, and by your student code of ethics.

Our notion of a correct way of doing things, which we see in our desire and need for policies on campus, reminds us that there is a constant, objective moral dimension to our lives. This moral dimension, which is evident in every culture, exists so that good and kindness can thrive. When we stand for truth, even by simply keeping our eyes on our own work, we are not supporting an abstract idea or general set of rules. We are standing in support of a Creator whose nature is true and who desires truth and goodness in His creation. When a friend walks in during the previews to a movie, you might stand to show her where you are and that you're glad she came. Standing, however uncomfortable to you and annoying to those around you, will bring her into where you are, into the area that you are sitting and around the people nearest you. You understand that her presence will add something, namely joy, to your situation, so you're willing to stand.

When you stand up for truth by adhering to God's ordinances and your campus policies during college, you're saying, "I understand the real state of this campus. I know that we need His presence here, around my friends, professors, and other students." You know there is a deep need for Truth and you are willing to stand, even in small ways, in support so that others might see your relationship to Him and be drawn in.

Truth Needs Grace

While helping out with a youth group as an undergraduate, the youth leader approached me and said, "Trevor, I'm glad you care more about your relationship with students than you do about teaching them deep theological truths." I was surprised by the comment. I cared deeply about God's Word and about the students. To me, genuine relationship with students was a deep theological truth. Relationship was needed so that I could communicate truth through our friendship. When the time was right, they listened to the tough stuff.

Grace, God's continual, humble desire for relationship with us, is expressed through His love for us. This grace relationship encourages us, and it motivates and inspires us to do right. Without it, we wouldn't be able to approach truth; truth would only push us away and show us our inadequate nature. Grace must always be present when dealing with truth; it pulls us in and allows us to change. Listen to John Bunyan's brilliant illumination of truth and grace in *Pilgrim's Progress*:

> Then he took him by the hand, and led him into a very large parlour that was full of dust, because never swept; the which, after he had reviewed a little while, the Interpreter called for a man to sweep: now when he began to sweep, the dust began so abundantly to fly about, that Christian had almost therewith been choked. Then said the Interpreter to a damsel that stood by 'Bring hither water, and sprinkle the room', which when she had done, was swept and cleansed with pleasure.
>
> *Christian*: Then said Christian, What means this?
>
> *Interpreter*: The Interpreter answered: This parlour is the heart of man that was never sanctified by the sweet grace of the Gospel; that dust is his original sin, and inward corruptions that have defiled the whole man. He that began to sweep at first is the Law, but she that brought water, and did sprinkle it, is the Gospel.[5]

What a compelling illustration! When talking truth with others, sprinkle your conversation with grace. Allow truth to stir the dust of their hearts, but don't leave them unsettled. Understand deep reality, and show kindness by speaking "truth in love," so the heart can experience cleansing and contentment.[6] Don't water down the truth (Jude 1:4); just flavor it with grace by treating others the way that you want to be treated.

Presenting truth in grace allows others to take a deep look at their current state and ways of thinking and then gives them the freedom to grow. Grace sees and answers the deepest needs of humanity. The Pharisees didn't understand truth because they lacked grace. We, like the would-be stone throwers, can engage all of our own logic and still come up short on our quest for being right. Because truth is spiritual, we must have Grace to help us see the dimension in our choices and interactions. We search for truth, but only He can illuminate it and show us how best to make it a part of our lives.

In your conversations, debates, and presentations as a college student, present truth in such a way that it addresses the hearts and the minds in your audience.

Start Now

Plant seeds of truth now. In 10 years, when someone asks you about college, conversations about the nature of reality and the existence of God will stir up. You'll remember the paper you wrote with the intent of persuading your professor to experience truth. You'll remember how others responded in biology when you asked the professor "How can something come from nothing?" or "How can organic life come from inorganic material?" or "If that's the case, then where does information come from?" You'll remember that your heart, actions, words, and thoughts worked in unison, each complementing the other. You'll remember that truth was maximized because you delivered it with grace. If nothing else, see the real state of our world during college and speak because, as C.S. Lewis urges, "Good philosophy must exist, if for no other reason, because bad philosophy needs to be answered."[7]

In an introductory communication course, I heard a student give a speech about the importance and benefits of returning to a transcendental perspective in society. He said, "To say there is no such thing as absolute truth is to make an absolute statement." If you make that claim (there is no such thing as absolute truth), you've said that you understand all truth, and the absolute truth is that there is no truth. An apparent contradiction! In an attempt to make an historical argument, he also engaged the class with the idea that societies work best when they make moral decisions, choices motivated by belief in the One who made the moral law because this brings clarity to thought and action. He also reminded students that absolute truth exists in mathematics $(1 + 1 = 2)$, in physics (drop an apple and it will fall), and in the social sciences (valuing and taking care of others will keep society from becoming self-destructive). He challenged the class to see the reality of and the need for a spiritual perspective because the state of our country depended on it.

There is a need, an exigency, for truth that requires a response. Too many Christian students shy away from the courses that don't line up with their beliefs. Instead of learning how to invite others to experience reality, they avoid the courses and students that need them most. They stick with the required readings instead of searching out God's perspective on their courses and major.

We should do our best to learn and communicate our Judeo-Christian perspective, the heritage that 106 of the first 108 American universities were built upon, in our course work and presentations because truth is a name, not a generic noun.[8] If we will ask Him to display His power on our campuses, and do our part by living with grace and truth, He will transform the lives of students, faculty, staff, and dark situations.

Truth, ultimate Reality, would continue to exist if we weren't here, and can fully be pursued and understood only when we deal with our most compelling choice.

try Reality

1. Learn what God's ordinances are for the areas that you're studying. What is His perspective on your major? If you don't learn and present the truth about your subject, who will?
2. Your papers, your presentations, and your conversations can be filled with God's principles, and they don't have to sound forced.
3. Be spiritually active on campus by living with moral excellence. Serve on your campus judicial board or student government or seek out a leadership position.

4. Ask God ahead of time, not just in the moment of crisis, to keep you honest during tempting situations (i.e., the professor leaves the room for a minute during an exam).
5. Learn how to use references effectively. Take a course or visit your campus's writing lab to learn how to properly use APA, MLA, or your professors' preferred citation style.
6. When confronting others, use grace and truth. I heard a counselor refer to it as an empathy sandwich: Be encouraging before you say the tough stuff and then conclude with encouragement. Only God's Spirit can change hearts.

Chapter 8

A Compelling Choice

CAMPUS LIFE IS OFTEN scripted. We don't just show up and create a student culture. We show up and receive it. When you were younger, what images did you have of being a college student? Where did you get these ideas?

A lot of our life is scripted. We regularly have "a general idea of how some event should play out or unfold."[1] Why else would a 9-year-old spit before he steps up to the plate to bat? He's seen the script. When you go to a basketball game with friends, you know the template to follow: you meet up before the game, walk to the arena, find your way to the student section, find a seat, wait for the game to start, shout for your team as they make their way onto the court, stand most of the game, distract the other team as they're shooting free throws, high five your neighbor after a great play, discuss the logistics of the game, have a predictable response based on the outcome, wait in line as you leave the arena. The game itself is unpredictable, but some of our responses and our actions during the game are scripted.

Campus life works the same way. You walk into a lecture hall, find your seat, pull out some paper, listen to the professor, take notes, ask a question or two, daydream, listen to the homework assignment, get up and leave. You have a general idea of what to expect and what you think your response should be during a college lecture. Walk into a fraternity house on Thursday night, and you'll be prompted to follow a social script. If nothing else, you'll feel awkward if you're the only one not carrying a cup or glass bottle. The scripts aren't new; they're the same ones students have been following for years.

If you are going to live in freedom during college, then learn to re-write and turn down some of the scripts that you're handed. It doesn't take a Ph.D. in cultural studies to know what negative scripts you will be given during college; they're the same ones you've been offered many times before. They'll just come at you from a different direction and with a heightened intensity: the flesh-driven script, the eye-lust script, and the script that encourages you to keep your focus on yourself and others instead of God.[2] If you want freedom and to live your purpose during college, then recognize dark scripts, make a break from them, and live out your true story.

Building Blocks

Your destiny is situated on the building blocks of your decisions. As a student, establish a secure foundation for your future by making solid choices now. We make thousands of decisions a day and it is up to us to make excellent ones. It's the seemingly small ones that propel you into your full potential. Some students forfeit their best because they never make the distinction between permissible and beneficial (1 Corinthians 6:12). If you will go from making good, to great, to excellent decisions, you'll have an unmatched college experience.

Steven Covey says, "Between stimulus and response, there is a space. In that space is our power to choose our response. In our response lies our growth and our freedom."[3] Another driver cuts you off on your way to a friend's house. Your response? A stressed-out roommate yells at you. Your response? If you will choose the right belief about your circumstance you can choose freedom and growth when conflict arises, and this response will inspire others to try a higher response.

If you want to mature and to live up to your potential, get a feel for how and why you make the decisions you do. William Perry, after conducting a longitudinal study of students, created a model of student intellectual and ethical development during college. He noticed how students' patterns of thinking change. His model can give us personal insight into where we are with how we make decisions.[4]

When a student begins college, he views the world in opposites (everything has a stark black-and-white contrast). For him, different viewpoints usually cause a lot of personal discomfort (which is why some academic advisors would suggest he wait until his sophomore year before taking a philosophy course). He might see those in authority, a professor for instance, as the primary source he should rely on for answers.

As he progresses in his decision making, he begins to consider multiple perspectives. He realizes that other people have their own way of seeing things. He starts to understand their ideas without feeling personally threatened by their views. He begins to wonder about his own sources of truth. He asks: Why do I believe what I do? Who has influenced my beliefs? Is what I believe true?

As he continues in his studies and interaction with others, he begins to think in a more analytical way. He starts to evaluate ideas and decisions of himself and others. This higher level of thinking, however, brings with it the potential for intellectual resistance and confusion. Out of fear and uncertainty, he might try to digress to the safety of an earlier level of thinking. He might go back to just accepting things because someone told him to, instead of learning to do his own research and develop his own convictions.

If he makes it beyond his confusion with the fact that people have their own beliefs, he will begin to make his own commitments based on personal convictions about behavior, relationships, and ideas. This time, unlike when he started college, the commitments are based on evaluating multiple perspectives and ideas, rather than believing the first person who offers a perspective. Now he seeks advice from multiple counselors. He does his own research.

Being at this place in our thinking is valuable because it allows us to engage our own minds while utilizing helpful points from other perspectives. The danger that is always present, however, is that we can get confused about truth as we listen to competing voices. We forget that absolute answers do exist and that sharp contrast of ideas is often needed. When we get to this place of thinking, we see that humility is not an option, it is a must.

If you are on a road trip and you pass some gum to a friend in the back seat, how fast is the gum traveling? Two miles per hour? If a bystander, alongside the road, watches you pass the gum, how fast would he say? 60 miles per hour? Because there are different planes of reality at work, an outside viewpoint must be taken into account when making a decision on how fast the gum is travelling.

Recognizing the complexity of our decisions and the effects of their consequences should lead us to know that we must get perspective higher than our own. As a college student, because you are going through significant cognitive changes, it is critical to recognize that you have a continual need for God to guide you. If it takes multiple viewpoints to understand how fast the pack of gum is traveling, then think about how important it is to go beyond our own limited perspective concerning our daily decisions. We should seek insightful perspectives, but no voice should be as important to us as the voice that sees all of reality.

try Peace

We have gray areas in our decisions. Why? Because we cannot see or hear all of reality. Because we're flawed creatures. We know that "A well-developed conscience does not translate, necessarily, into a morally courageous life. Nor do well-developed powers of philosophical thinking and moral analysis necessarily translate into an everyday willingness to face down the various evils of this world."[5] The apostle Paul put it, "For in my inner being I delight in God's law; but I see another law at work in the members of my body, waging war against the law of my mind and making me a prisoner of the law of sin at work within my members. What a wretched man I am! Who will rescue me from this body of death?" (Romans 7:22-24).

The living out of a principled life, a benefit to everyone, is something that we all face. We carry within us the idea that there is a correct way to live; we just never fully carry it out. That's why our parents used to tell us to "straighten up," and then moments later we were misbehaving again. We know that there is a standard, but we are unable to keep it because of our sinful nature. Everyone knows of something they should have done but didn't. Or should not have done but did. This self-knowledge, prompted by guilt, simply reminds us that we are imperfect and are in need spiritually.

I had a professor who always brought a much needed perspective on human behavior to his classes. Towards the end of one of his lectures, he said, "What if nothing works?" What if we continue to make our legal and criminal justice system more efficient, but it changes nothing? His long pause let the question sink in. Then he said, "Give me some reasons that people are in prison." A girl on the front row called out, "murder." "Could we say that anger motivated the behavior?" he responded. Someone else spoke up, "stealing." He replied, "Could we call the motive covetousness?" Before he finished his lecture about human behavior, he had written on the board seven areas that stain all of our lives:

- Pride
- Lust
- Covetousness
- Anger
- Gluttony
- Envy
- Sloth

He finished his lecture with silence. He didn't have to say anything else. We got the message.

Notice that Paul did not ask, "*What* will rescue me?" He knew that no code of ethics or social system could change the reality of his struggle. No motivation within himself nor outside institution could force him to want to do right. He said "*Who* will" because he knew someone with higher ability needed to help him. He knew that his nature was flawed. Because he was willing to do what it took to make things right he looked to the One with a nature higher than his own. The same One with whom Professor Lewis challenges us to clarify our standing:

> Jesus…told people that their sins were forgiven…This makes sense only if He really was the God whose laws are broken and whose love is wounded in every sin…I am trying here to prevent anyone from saying the really foolish thing that people often say about Him: 'I'm ready to accept Jesus as a great moral teacher, but I don't accept his claim to be God.' That is the one thing we must not say. A man who was merely a man and said the sort of things Jesus said would not be a great moral teacher. He would either be a lunatic—on a level with a man who says he is a poached egg— or else he would be the Devil of Hell. You can shut Him up for a fool, you can spit at Him and kill Him as a demon; or you can fall at His feet and call Him Lord and God. But let us not come with any patronizing nonsense about His being a great human teacher. He has not left that open to us. He did not intend to.[6]

The compelling choice that is always before us is to believe Jesus is who He said He was, to believe that He has the supernatural ability to change us and to calm the struggle within. When we give our life to the Counselor-Creator, He guides us in how best to live by creating in us a spiritual heart that is designed to listen to His voice. This is a fundamental difference between Christianity and all other religions. Religion offers a moral code to follow, a moral ladder to climb, but Jesus offers the internal equipment with which to climb. Beyond higher moral ground, He makes us right with God. The only way to live at the "rock higher than I" is the death of self and the rebirth of the Christ in its place.[7] To live out your best during and after college requires deciding where you stand with the only person who can set your will free to choose excellence. When you know Him, you are set free because He changes your inner person. You are given a new nature, one that is prone to seek out and do good, one that is designed to fulfill the true moral standard. We try higher simply because He motivates us do so.

Oswald Chambers writes,

"The golden rule to follow to obtain spiritual understanding is not one of intellectual pursuit, but one of obedience. If a person wants scientific knowledge, then intellectual curiosity must be his guide. But if he desires knowledge and insight into the teachings of Jesus Christ, he can only obtain it through obedience. If spiritual things seem dark and hidden to me, then I can be sure that there is a point of disobedience somewhere in my life. Intellectual darkness is the result of ignorance, but spiritual darkness is the result of something that I do not intend to obey."[8]

In the center of every decision there is a right way. The right way is to surrender the choice to God. To believe Him when He says He will be our guide. If you will "try to discern what is pleasing" to Him, He will show you the best path to take (Ephesians 5:10, ESV). He will teach you what you need to learn during college even when things seem gray. He can guide your mind to the right conclusions as you study, think, research, and pursue wisdom.

How you go about making decisions will change during college. You, not your teachers or parents, are responsible for your learning and for consequences. When dealing with the area between a stimulus and your response, ensure that you make the right choice. **Stimulus**... offer the decision to God, ask for His direction, search Scripture, get sound advice... and then **Respond**.

The foundation you will have when you make spirit-motivated decisions will be unshakeable. Do not neglect the fact that you can know and discern right and wrong during college; look to the One who is truth so he can "... instruct you and teach you in the way you should go" (Psalm 32:8).

try Compelling Choice

1. Your beliefs are the building blocks of your decisions. Guard your heart and mind at all cost during college.
2. If you want to live free, then be selective about the social settings in which you allow yourself to be. Some personalities and social scripts are better off never crossing.

3. If college is a play, which script are you reading from? Why?
    Why not live above some social scripts? Why not make people
    question your decisions because they are contrary to the
    normal? Why not bring a helping hand on the Sabbath? Why
    not, like Daniel, purpose to do something simple yet profound?
    Remember that it is always individuals like Martin Luther or
    William Wilberforce who, inspired by God, write new social
    scripts and bring positive change.
4. Recognize that your decisions have a spiritual dimension to
    them. When faced with choice, submit the decision to the One
    who promised to guide you during college. As you continue
    to be obedient, He will give you the insight you need to make
    excellent decisions.

Spirit-Filled Learning

I have never let my schooling interfere with my education.
—Mark Twain[1]

IF YOU WILL FOCUS on learning and not just on making the grade during college, you'll take your knowledge further. You will be the one person who takes an idea to a new level. You'll take opportunities that others pass by. You'll see where others don't.

College is less about how much time you spend studying and more about how much learning you engage yourself in while studying. You can study for hours with little progress toward learning the material. I once asked a pediatric dentist how he managed to be successful as an undergraduate. He said he spaced his classes out, and after each lecture he would immediately review his notes and read back through the material in the book. While he reinforced important course information, he also engaged himself in mastering the material. This strategy worked for him because it took him to new levels of learning.

What level of learning have you reached with your current courses? Take a look at Benjamin Bloom's six levels of learning:

1. Remember
2. Understand
3. Apply
4. Analyze
5. Evaluate
6. Create [2]

If you are at the first level of learning in a Spanish course, then you're able to recognize and recall information. You should be able to memorize new words for your tests. As you progress higher, you will begin to understand the structure and grammar rules of the language, and you'll be able to explain what you are learning to a friend. As you continue higher, you'll be able to critique how you and others speak and write. By the end of the course, you could consider a study abroad trip to a destination where you would create language with others.

Here's another example. Do you ever play trivia games? Do you watch game shows that test your knowledge? These types of games typically use questions to test the facts you know. They measure your span of knowledge. You might be asked, "Who was the 16th president of the United States?" or "What is the oldest college in the U.S.?" While important, facts are lower levels of learning. They are simply the building blocks to understanding and insight. What tone did Abraham Lincoln set as the leader of our nation? Answering this question involves a higher level of thinking. Understanding how he led our country and his motivation for decision-making is another step higher. Incorporating his leadership principles into your own life is a step even higher.

Your mind is able to take information and use it to create. When you store up knowledge, by remembering and understanding, you allow your mind to take that information and to move you to a place of illumination, to an "ah ha" moment. Even when you're asleep, your mind works on creating solutions to problems based on the information you've given it. Ben Carson, Professor and Director of Pediatric Neurosurgery at Johns Hopkins, understood this phenomenon when he described, in his book *Think Big*, his use of Herman Helmholtz's process of scientific discoveries:

1. *Saturation*
    He conducted research, finding out everything he could learn on the subject.

2. *Incubation*
    This is the reflective time, the thinking and mulling over what he had learned through research.

3. *Illumination*
    Helmholz faithfully gave his full concentration to satura-
    tion and incubation. Then, he said, he arrived at a sudden
    solution.[3]

When you store up knowledge, even if you don't consider yourself creative, your mind will take that information and use it to
create. Your mind will use knowledge to help you solve a problem,
write a paper, give an impromptu speech, or seize an opportunity
that others pass up. Even students who are deciding on a major can
use Helmholz's model.

You can:

1. (Saturate) Research all of the majors and departments on
campus by talking with professors and other students, reading the
Catalog of Studies, and studying handouts from departments. You
can also take introductory courses and classes that seem interesting
and challenging. You can talk with an advisor about your options.
Or ask a professor about what's involved in a major and what some
of the graduates from that department are doing now.

2. (Incubate) Reflect on your options by weighing the pros and
cons. You can decide which degree plan aligns with your priorities
and talents (*e.g.*, time frame for completing a degree, intensity of
studies, fit with ability, motivation level for studying material).

3. (Illuminate) Allow God to illuminate which path to take. You
can listen to Him about your best options as you recognize your
motivation to study a subject and identify your strengths.

Motivated to Major

Your choice to take a certain elective says something about who
you are. Your desire to pursue a major reveals something about
your disposition, about your talents. You have been given a unique
way to process information and a unique way to apply it to your life.
You see the topics in class in a way that only you can. When you
are motivated to major in a field of study, not only will the information be intriguing, but you will be able to take it places that no

others can because they are not you. Your past, your beliefs, and the unique "you" all work together to color how you see and apply knowledge.

I had a professor explain it using C.G. Jung's *Synchronization.* When it came time to start on our research papers, she cautioned us to select a topic with great care. She felt that our topic selection was very much connected to who we were and our place in life. When I look back at my topics and research papers, I see what she was talking about. My topics, how I developed my arguments, and my writing style, all revealed something about my personality and my unique calling—that is, my desire and potential to motivate others to see the importance of the spiritual dimension to life. Listening to God about our courses and which information to devote the most time to is deeply important.

When you find your "sweet spot," you will notice that the information changes you. Your mind will grasp it in a way that is different from other material. Your determination to study longer, think deeper, and apply what you have learned will grow. I talked with a student once who described her experiences as, "It just made sense when I started into my social work courses. When it came time to take the essay tests, I had something to say. My mind could wrap around the ideas, apply them, and expand on them." She came into college knowing that she might like to be a counselor someday, but she was unsure of a major. She talked with a friend who was attending a graduate program in counseling who suggested she look into social work, so she decided to take an intro course. It was a fit. While she was exploring her options, God placed someone in her life to help point her in the right direction. Some call it synchronization; we know it is providence.

God will help you make the right decision concerning your major (Psalm 25:12). Even more important is the reality that God can use any major you pick to help you fulfill His purpose for you. He has already placed talent within you, so college is merely an opportunity to help you grow and gain knowledge and skills that will complement your talent. College is a place where God can illuminate your strengths, your unique mission, and point you in the initial direction of where to use that talent. I asked a student once about the difference between his math courses and his history courses. He said math just clicked for him. He liked history and could do well in it, but it didn't have the same effect on his mind that math did. So he decided to go with math as a major. History was interesting, but math was motivating.

Knowledge is never neutral. Ideas always influence you. You will be changed by what you place in your mind, so listen to God on which studies to pursue. Learn from every course that you take. Each elective, general education class, and major course can add dimension to your thinking. See the good in knowledge, but recognize and look for the material that you are most drawn to and capable of learning. God built within each of us talents, and during college we can discover these unique strengths by finding and staying close to the information that we enjoy learning and applying. Remember that there are levels to learning. When you store up knowledge and reflect on what you have been studying, you allow your mind, guided by God, to move you to a higher place of learning. A place of insight and creativity.

To get the most out of college, be teachable. Don't be like those who are "ever hearing but never understanding" or "seeing but never perceiving" (Matthew 13:14). Instead, have a sensitive heart, one that "hears the word and understands it" so that you can produce "a hundred, sixty or thirty times what was sown" during your college years (Matthew 13:23).

try Higher Learning

1. How can you take your mind to its full potential?
   a. Esteem God above all else (Proverbs 9:10),
   b. Listen to His instruction (Proverbs 8:33), and
   c. Do what He tells you (Proverbs 9:6).
2. Focus on your academic strengths and the areas that God motivates you to improve. We can do well in many subjects (give someone enough time and he can comprehend a variety of

majors), but ask God to guide you into the areas in which you can excel. Let Him show you where your true strength and potential lie. Ask Him, do your part by storing up knowledge, and He will guide you.

3. Learn how you learn. Take a learning inventory. Talk with a professor, a learning specialist, or your academic counselor about learning styles and about tips for studying for courses and tests (*e.g.*, multiple choice, true/false, short answer, essay, problem-based).

4. Use Helmholtz's model with your courses and with Scripture. Learn all you can each week about your course work and what God says about the topic. Reflect on what He is teaching you, and watch as He illuminates new principles and how to apply them.

5. See *try Exploring Your Major* for more tips on deciding on a major.

Chapter
10

Spiritual Motivation

So I was afraid and went out and hid your talent in the ground.
—Matthew 25:25

ARE YOU USING YOUR talent? Or hiding it? Motivation is choosing to make the most of the gifts that God has entrusted you with. It's having an unrelenting desire to see your dreams become reality. To do your best in college because you know it will stir up your potential.

We are built with deep reservoirs of motivation. These storehouses are just waiting to provide us with the energy we need to answer our unique calling. With the right perspective, we can be continually refreshed by these deep pools of motivation.

When you are internally motivated, no one has to force you to study; you just do. You enjoy learning and the good that comes from understanding. Students are considered internally motivated if they—during free time and without being told—return to a project that they had been previously working on. Research shows that these kids use their free time to do an extra problem, to check out a new book from the library, or to further investigate an idea that they heard about in class.[1] It is no surprise when these kids succeed; they have been storing up knowledge and working hard to discover their thinking potential. What a great way to live. Your success during college is a function of your internal motivation, your willingness to take risks with growing, and to keep striving even when you have not been successful before.

Some students require a bit more external motivation than others. They need a push to get them started. External incentives can enhance motivation, but they're no substitute for relying on internal flame. I knew an English professor who loved to write, but it was still a chore for him. To get himself motivated, he would write a paragraph every morning before he would allow himself a cup of coffee. He would reward himself with coffee. His incentive helped keep his internal desire and love for writing going strong and moving forward.

Motivation is the capacity you have for action. In many ways, it resembles the concept of energy that science applies to matter, the capacity to do work. Motivation, like energy, can come from different sources for different purposes. The problem is not whether or not you are motivated (because everyone is motivated), but rather the concern is the source of your motivation and the direction in which you are applying your energy. We can understand and rely on our most powerful motivation when we understand our spiritual source.

Right Source, Right Motive

If you want to have the right motive during college, then choose the right source. The right source and motive keep you from being distracted as you discover your destiny. Thomas Kelly says, "The outer distractions of our interests reflect an inner lack of integration in our own selves. We are trying to be several selves at once without all our selves being organized by a single, mastering Life within us."[2] As Christians, we have a single source of motivation, so we don't have to get distracted by things and relationships that waste our life during college. Our continual source of motivation is the One who trades guilt with love and who creates within us a spiritual motive. It is our Salvation that causes our internal fire to burn higher and hotter:

> Then I saw in my dream that the Interpreter took Christian by the hand, and led him into a place where was a fire burning against a

wall, and one standing by it always, casting much water upon it to quench it: yet did the fire burn higher and hotter.

Then said Christian, 'What means this?'

The Interpreter answered, 'This fire is the work of grace that is wrought in the heart; he that casts water upon it, to extinguish and put it out, is the Devil: but in that thou seest the fire, notwithstanding, burn higher and hotter, thou shalt also see the reason of that. So he had him about to the backside of the wall, where he saw a man with a vessel of oil in his hand, of the which he did also continually cast, but secretly, into the fire.

Then said Christian, 'What means this?'

The Interpreter answered, 'This is Christ, who continually, with the oil of his grace, maintains the work already begun in the heart...'[3]

When you have the Christ in your life, He maintains your inner fire by fueling it with the oil of grace. We can overcome everyday challenges because we have a continual supply of spiritual strength. The psalmist says, "...therefore God, your God, has set you above your companions by anointing you with the oil of joy" (Psalm 45:7). God, our joy, is our strength. When others run out of motivation to do right, we keep running because we have a supernatural supply. We are motivated to be our best because we have a spirit-filled perspective, an outlook that places the entirety of our life in circumference of the single, mastering Life.

During my junior year, I learned from physical chemistry that the structure of an element determines its function. I'm not sure the number of ways the concept plays out in chemistry (I made a D in the course), but I found how it applied to my life. I realized that, like the chemical world, how I structured my life would determine my function. How I managed myself, my time, and my thinking would influence how far I would go, and how I would be used. A life centered on truth and kindness would enhance my joy and effectiveness.

College Motive

I have talked with many students who feel they need to work on their motivation in order to succeed in college. They are accustomed to their parents or high school teachers being their source of motivation. Now in college, they are primarily responsible for motivating themselves. They've not asked themselves the hard questions. They're not even sure what their motive is for continuing their education. They're just here because it is the next thing to do after high school.

If you do not understand your motive or the source of your strength during college, then someone else will be able to persuade you to use your energy in ways that diminish your potential and distract you from your best. If you want to increase your motivation, then ask God to give you new desires. When you are tempted to wait for others to get you motivated to study, ask Him to give you a desire to work hard, and to be in charge of yourself. Now is the best time to get started creating new habits of hard work.

I like what brothers, teenagers at the time, Alex and Brett Harris say about motivation. In their book, *Do Hard Things*, they list "Five Kinds of Hard" that we should all be engaged in:

- things that take you outside your comfort zone—taking risks to grow
- things that go beyond what's expected or required—pursuing excellence
- things that are too big to accomplish alone—dreaming and daring big
- things that don't earn an immediate payoff—being faithful and choosing integrity
- things that go against the cultural norm—taking a stand for what is right [4]

Choosing to grow. Pursuing excellence. Dreaming and daring big. Living with integrity. Standing for what is right. That is the best way to live during college. By looking to God and taking the initiative to do hard things, you will learn something from every course and every professor. You'll leave college reaching higher than you ever imagined.

Whether you attend a research-based university, a four-year college, an open-door community college, or a for-profit institution, you have something to add to and learn from that environment. A diversity of institutions is needed to meet the needs of a diverse student population, and a diversity of majors is needed to meet the diverse needs of society. You have a purpose during and after college. Living it means you are listening to God's Spirit, your source of motivation, in the details of your life.

try Spiritual Motivation

1. Ask God to create in you an unrelenting desire to fulfill His purpose for your life. Let His desires be your motivation.
2. Find out what motivates you. Like my professor with his coffee, how can you make things you enjoy work for you?
3. What are your spiritual gifts? Your motivation is immeasurable when you are relying on the Spirit to work through you.
4. Learn to eat for performance, not just pleasure. Keep active. Get sleep. These three principles will increase your energy and help you feel better which will help you clarify your motivation.
5. Get around energetic, balanced people. Mark Victor Hansen, co-author of the *Chicken Soup for the Soul* series and an extremely motivated individual, says he has listened to more than 10,000 audiocassettes while driving, and he continually seeks out positive, motivating mentors to have in his life.[5] We always have the option of keeping ourselves motivated by being around the right people and information.

Go to the Ant

I TALKED WITH A STUDENT once who had experienced some trouble with her first semester courses. She said, "I thought I understood time management and even my finances before I came to college...and now I see it's not the case."

Like many students, she had to re-learn how to manage her life during college. She had come to the realization that her previous routine worked because she had depended almost entirely on her parents to set the tone for how to get things done. While the principles her family had been teaching her were beneficial and right, she had not internalized them and applied them on her own.

If you will internalize, through practice, the principles of the ant during college, you will take your potential further. Ants are masters of taking small steps to prepare for the future. Their test is the coming winter, so they know they must get ready. Working hard to accomplish their task is built within them, and they labor to make their internal mission an external reality. There is no doubt that ants will accomplish their goal; they are too busy staying focused.

Ants are in a constant state of preparation. They realize what is coming next, and they prepare. They do not need someone asking, "Shouldn't you be studying for Wednesday's test?" They have "...no commander, no overseer," yet an ant "...stores its provisions in summer and gathers its food at harvest" (Proverbs 6:7-8).

On occasion, I run into ant-like students. They think ahead. They recognize the purpose in what they're currently doing. They know their present action is taking them to a future destination. They pace themselves. They take small steps on assignments. They work ahead. They motivate themselves. They work in teams. They store up their energy for the tough weeks ahead.

Ant-like students break assignments into small pieces. They know that their best learning is made by consistent study, not cramming. Instead of procrastinating until the weekend before a term paper is due, they do it in parts. Their schedule to finish a paper might look like this:

Week 1:
1. Decide on a research topic.
2. Narrow topic to a workable idea.
3. Ask professor after class if it sounds like a good idea.

Week 2:
1. Find 5 articles that address my topic.
2. Find 2 books that address my topic.
3. Review my sources/references.
4. Create a thesis/outline for my paper.
5. Ask professor if outline looks good.

Week 3:
1. Write 1-2 pages a day.
2. Finish rough draft.

Week 4:
1. Review rough draft and re-write.
2. Take paper to the writing center to have someone read through it.
3. Make revisions.
4. Turn paper in.

If you are going to be successful during and after college then look for small ways to improve your schedule and habits. Students who live the principle of the ant—taking consistent, small steps— use it in every area of their lives. I took a one-credit-hour aerobics and weight training course my sophomore year, and the teacher made us keep a weekly log of the food that we ate. One of the seniors in the course, a defensive lineman who wanted to lose some weight, also had a part-time job at a local fried chicken restaurant. By keeping the journal for class, he realized that he was eating fried chicken much more than he had thought. From this awareness, he didn't stop eating the chicken, but he did start taking the skin off. Before the semester was over, he had lost 25 pounds. By looking for small ways to improve, he found big results.

Time Perspective

Successful students have a unique perspective of time. They understand that time is one of their most valuable resources and tools. They know that today is going to cost them a day of their life, so they make it worth the price. They make time work for them by staying ahead.

Did you know that many ROTC (Reserve Officers' Training Corps) students are required to create an academic plan? As part of their scholarship requirement, they have to map out how they will complete their degree in four years. They have to put some good thought into how they're going to sequence their courses. They make sure that they will have the prerequisites done so they can go on to advanced courses. They know that their extra time and summers will be filled with training, so they schedule time with an advisor to plan ahead. Many of them are not natural planners, but it's something that they are learning to master.

To effectively manage the life God gave you, realize you have a need to see time the way that He does. For many, the verse "A little sleep a little slumber and poverty will pounce on you..." is enough to get them up and moving around (Proverbs 6:10-11). A renewing of the mind always gets us motivated. If you will change your perspective, get around organized people, practice success strategies, and reflect on how you have been spending your life, you will go further during college. If we will just ask God, He will "Teach us to number our days aright, that we may gain a heart of wisdom" (Proverbs 90:12).

I talk to students every semester who miss out on enjoying the process of learning because of anxiety or depression. Because of the pain and stress involved with growing, they're never content while in school. Before they know it, their four years are over. They come to class, and all they think about is, "I can't wait to get out of here and get on with my day." They "can't wait until summer," so they can start enjoying being a college student. Being balanced during college means you can enjoy the challenge of the process.

You can make the most of each class and get the most out of each semester because you're a content person. See the value in the knowledge and in the experience so that you can make the most of every situation. Plan ahead so you can have the freedom to be content. Remember that learning and growing into your potential takes time. A student once asked the president of his school if there was a course he could take that was shorter than the one prescribed. "Oh yes," replied the president, "but it depends on what you want to be. When God wants to make an oak, He takes a hundred years, but when He wants to make a squash, it only takes six months."[1] Having a realistic view of time and its importance is essential to making the most of college.

If you want to remain in good academic standing and enjoy the process, then do what it takes to make it happen. Learn from the ants who are experts at being consistent workers, self-starters, effective communicators, team-focused participants, and strong finishers. If your Creator says, "Go to the ant, you sluggard; consider its ways and be wise," then take Him up on it, and buy an ant farm. Set it up in your dorm, and watch and learn. By studying ants, you will learn the art of successful living. You've made the decision to be in school, so now it's time to manage that choice through discipline.

try Ant-Principles

1. See the value in your time and the brevity of your life.
2. Create an academic plan so that you can visualize your college career. See *Try A College Plan, Leadership Plan, and Plan Weekly* for tips on creating your unique plan. As you make plans,

remember to be flexible with your decisions because you may be taken a different way.

3. See *try* Focused Motivation! for tips on breaking assignments into workable parts, and *try* 5 Reasons—College Students Succeed for tips on staying in good academic standing.

4. Will you choose to be content every day during college? If so, then give your experience to God, pray continually, prepare the best you can, and contentment will become a reality for you.

Communicate!

All I realize is that the presentation is merely a conversation between me and the other people I'm giving the speech to.[1]
—A college student

AT A RECENT FAMILY reunion, my cousin came up to me and remarked, "I read what you said about communication during college, and I think you're right about it." My Mom had brought a copy of my newly completed dissertation on communication and college students and set it out for our family to see. My cousin picked it up and flipped to the back to read the recommendations. As a junior in college, he wished that he'd learned earlier the importance and benefits of effective communication with professors, staff, and students.

Solomon tells us, "The heart of the wise instructs his mouth, and adds persuasiveness to his lips."[2] Students who combine intellect, emotional understanding, credibility, and spiritual insight write excellent papers, work well in teams, and give convincing speeches. Communication, which involves sending and receiving messages, can help you carry out the purpose within your heart as well as motivate others to strive toward excellence with you. Think of William Wallace, in the movie *Braveheart*, who led Scotland in a revolution to gain its independence. His words, his actions, and his life worked as one to inspire patriotism and to call others to fight for freedom. In savage warrior style and color he invoked his men, "Aye, fight and you may die. Run, and you'll live...at least a while. And dying in your beds, many years from now, would you be willin' to trade ALL the days, from this day to that, for one chance, just one chance, to come back here and tell our enemies that they may take our lives, but they'll never take...OUR FREEDOM."[3]

Communication will help you be the person of influence that God designed you to be. Asking your advisors questions, balancing your input during small groups, listening to professors, and learning to put your thoughts in writing will help you take your college experience further. Communication, which involves effectively listening, will also take you to new levels of learning, and it will help you pursue the mission that God has placed within you. Check any job advertisement section of the newspaper and you'll see that employers place speaking and listening skills among the most important abilities when hiring. Research also supports the fact that communication skills are essential to career upward mobility.[4] If you want to become a person of influence during college and increase your learning, then develop your unique communication potential.

Confident Communication

If you are apprehensive about talking or writing, you're not alone; for me, the intro speech class was one of my most dreaded courses, and I still get nervous about having others read what I've written. All college students experience some anxiety with presenting their ideas. The successful ones simply learn strategies to help them move beyond the emotions that keep them down. They realize that answering God's call means using their voice to help others. Even Billy Graham, an admired evangelist who preached to millions of people, experienced communication apprehension when he was in training to be a preacher. In his autobiography, *Just as I Am*, he writes about his first sermon,

> ...The congregation of about 40 included ranchers and cowboys in overalls and their women in cotton wash dresses. When the moment came to walk to the pulpit in the tiny Bostwick Baptist Church, my knees shook and perspiration glistened on my hands. I launched into sermon number one. It seemed to be over almost as soon as I got started, so I added number two. And number three. And eventually four. Then I sat down. Eight minutes—that was all it took to preach all four of my sermons! Was this the stuff of which those marvelous preachers at Florida Bible Institute were made of?[5]

Dr. Graham was supposed to give one sermon that night. Instead, thanks to his nerves, he gave four mini sermons in just 8 minutes; sermons he had prepared for future preaching opportunities. The inspiration from his story, as we know, is that he kept after it. He kept practicing. He didn't give up. He says that, "Believe it or not, though, when I got back to campus I felt that I had grown spiritually through the experience."[6] Although he wasn't as profound or polished as he hoped he would be, he knew that he was doing his best. He knew that his current ability had nothing to do with his future potential because he was willing to be used and developed by God.

Students who let fear get the best of them often avoid important communication situations, which means they miss out on the chance to improve during college. If you will choose to see your communication potential the way that God does, you will be able to make the most of every experience. If a professor knows that you're willing to lead, then you, instead of someone who avoids the situation, could be asked to help with a presentation or project. Students who learn to overcome their anxiety take advantage of communication opportunities. As a result, they improve their ability and effectiveness with people.

In doing the research for my dissertation, I asked more than seven hundred college students how they deal with communication apprehension. Here are some of their responses:

"I had to give a speech at my church in front of 350 people. I was nervous at the beginning just before they called my name. After getting on the stage to give my speech, I just remembered that the only person I was trying to impress was God..."

"Giving a speech in college. I just focused on a few people and acted like I was just talking to them."

"I visualize the situation and how it will be handled, then move on. There are worse things in life than having to communicate with someone or having to speak in public!"

"I had to give a sermonette for women's day at church, and I would have to take a few seconds when I felt anxiety coming on and just take a deep breath and focus on what I had prepared."

"The first time we had to present a paper in my Comp 2 class. It was a group presentation, and I was very nervous. As far as coping with the apprehension, I did well. I just thought of the classmates as friends I had known for quite a while. It also helped that my speech was about something I liked and was interested in. The excitement of being able to tell people what I knew and learned from the text overcame the apprehension. I was still nervous but not near as badly."

"I coped with it by realizing that I am bigger than my anxiety and got rid of it and pressed through my insecurity of what others would think."

"Giving speeches in class is always a little nerve-racking. I just go into the speech knowing I can and will do fine and just try to go into it as confident as possible since that usually reflects in the speech itself."

"I had to give a speech in class. To prepare for the speech, I researched and made a power point presentation. Then I practiced the speech by giving it to the wall. (It sounds silly, but it works!) It helped me gather my thoughts and retain the information that I wanted to present."

"I had to make a speech for my Upward Bound program at the end of the summer. I was anxious because I was explaining my years in my Upward Bound program and thanking our parents for giving us the freedom of participating in this program. I coped with my apprehension by realizing that all that I wrote was personal and that my speech was what I really needed to let everyone know."

"Being interviewed for a position and I just coped by taking deep breaths and reminding myself to listen intently to the questions. I prayed a lot and asked the Holy Spirit to help me to talk with clarity and correctly."[7]

If we choose to be like many of these students, then we will see communication as a conversation, not as a performance. We will speak from our convictions. We'll practice. We'll use a combination of strategies for dealing with stress. We'll communicate with creativity. We'll recognize the reality that our audience is responsible for listening, so they have some of the pressure on them too. We'll rely on the Holy Spirit to help us.

Don't let anxiety, a lack of confidence, or overconfidence keep you from developing essential speaking, writing, and listening skills during college. We all have the need and potential to improve, so be willing to take communication risks. If we can communicate with God, we can communicate with anyone. Ask Him, and He will begin to show you how to develop your own unique communication style. He can calm your heart and give you the words you need to succeed. Stop comparing your presentations and papers with others, and climb higher with your own style. You don't have to be overly fancy with your presentations and papers. Keep your heart pure and your speech simple. Even if you don't feel successful, keep after it, like Billy Graham did, because the experience will be used to help you grow spiritually.

try Communication

1. Remember that you are the message, so learn the scriptures that put communication in perspective:
    a. "Now go; I will help you speak and will teach you what to say" (Exodus 4:12).
    b. "My words come from an upright heart; my lips sincerely speak what I know" (Job 33:3).
    c. "Speak up for those who cannot speak for themselves, for the rights of all who are destitute" (Proverbs 31:8).
    d. "Kings take pleasure in honest lips; they value a man who speaks the truth" (Proverbs 16:13).
    e. "For in him you have been enriched in every way—in all your speaking and in all your knowledge—because our testimony about Christ was confirmed in you" (1 Corinthians 1:5-6).

2. Communication apprehension is not limited to public speaking, but can negatively affect your relationships, team work, writing, or even singing. Take a survey that measures your communication apprehension, and learn specific strategies for overcoming your anxiety.[8]

3. Seek out opportunities to improve your communication ability during college. Get involved in a public-speaking or drama program. Take English courses to build your vocabulary and writing ability. Use a small group to practice speaking up, or take a course on team building. Try leading a Bible study.

4. Remember to work on your verbal (public speaking, conversation, writing) and nonverbal (tone of voice, facial expression) communication; your message is effective when these are congruent.

5. Know your audience. If you are creating a relationship with your professors, ask them about their research. If you're at a university, then a big part of their day is spent pursuing new ideas. Treat your audience the way you prefer to be treated when in an audience.

6. Know your topic well. The better you know it, the better you'll feel about speaking on that topic.

7. See *Try a Checklist* for presentation tips.

Listening

As a college student, how often do you receive new information? Think about it: a majority of your time as a student is spent listening. In fact, most Americans spend 45% of their time listening, as compared to 9% writing, 30% speaking, and 16% reading.[9]

Although we spend much of our time listening, we're not necessarily great at it. Too often we hear people talking, but we do not actively listen to their message. We don't make it a point to engage our minds and hearts, so we miss out on the knowledge and dimension of what's being said. We imagine that we have the same picture in our mind as the one we're talking with, but in reality we miss what they were trying to share. We miss what our friend's heart was telling us when she called just to talk. We miss the depth of our professor's lecture because we let our wandering mind get the best of us.

Listening, a trait of God's, should be fully developed in our lives. The level of our success is directly related to this ability. In fact, research shows that employees who received listening instruction before they went to their computer technique training were more productive with the training and the application of their new knowledge.[10] Active listening is a learned ability. It can take us further in every area of life-learning.

Giving and receiving feedback is an important part of listening. Asking a question to clarify what a professor says will help your mind more fully use the information. Adjusting your grammar in a paper because of your teacher's feedback will only heighten your future writing ability. If you will benefit from all feedback by improving your work ethic and attitude, you won't waste energy replaying negative thoughts. However, not all feedback is worth giving mental real estate, so be discerning. Learn to respond well and you'll go further.

For the sake of being your best, develop your ability to listen actively during college. In a survey, 450 graduates of a business program marked listening as the number one training they wish they had received during college.[11] Don't wait around for training. Start your own program now. Ask God to help you listen well because if you're listening to Him during college, you're learning to listen to others.

try Listening

1. Tell yourself, "Ok, it's time to focus." Make your thoughts work for you by saying, "This professor and message are important. I know I can learn something from him."
2. Know why you are listening. To show compassion? To critique? To understand? For fun?
3. If you are listening to show compassion, avoid judging the person and her experience, and just let her know you're listening.
4. If you're critiquing a message, question the logic being used. What's the motive of the sender?

5. While in class, listen for main ideas or how the professor organizes the information. Try to understand her perspective and approach for delivering the message.
6. Use an effective approach for taking notes. Cornell University's note-taking system has been used by many students.[12]
7. Enjoy what you're learning. Make the information relevant to your life.

Relentless Relationship

BEFORE 1954, NO ATHLETE had run the mile in under four minutes. It was common knowledge that it could not be done.

After a failed attempt at the '52 Olympics, 25-year-old medical student, Roger Bannister, became the first man to run a mile in under four minutes. How did he do it? Relationships. Yes, he had the ability and he trained consistently, but to run faster and to run his best he had to rely on other runners. Two teammates went out before him to set the pace. Together they broke the record.[1]

This team energy is best known as synergy. It's the idea that, if you could lift 100 pounds by yourself, with the help of a friend you could lift 300 pounds together. That's 100 more than expected. With synergy, 1 + 1 is not always 2. Sometimes it's 3 or 4 or even 7. It's the exponential energy that relationship creates.

More than anything else, the quality of your relationships will influence your future. To be your best during college, you will need the right kinds of relationships. Iron relationships. Friends who won't compromise. Voices of encouragement and truth. Mentors of hope. Mature relationships that help you reach your potential.

Friends

Several friends I knew while growing up got lost in the mix of empty ideas and relationships during college. I remember sitting in a mid-sized auditorium as a senior. I had just finished listening to each debate team present its side. Scanning the audience to watch responses, I noticed a familiar face.

I thought I knew what his response would be; after all, I knew that we shared the same worldview when we were younger. Once the teams had finished, they asked the audience to show their support by exiting through the door next to the team that they supported. Exiting through the door on the right showed that you were in support of legalizing prostitution, while exiting to the left said you opposed the idea. As I made my way to the door on the left, it didn't take long to see that our line was short, while the door on the right had quite the gathering. Disappointed but not surprised because of the college environment, I noticed that my friend had eagerly made his way to the other door. My heart sank. As I watched him exit, I could tell by the expression on his face that a primary motive for his support was not because of the arguments used by the team but rather the pathos of being connected to a group of people. He chose to ignore truth for the sake of feeling connected.

Like many of you, I'm cautious around crowd Christians: students who talk big but have no game. The ones who are quick to say they are a Christian when asked about their faith or religion but are just as quick to have empty, vain behavior. Jesus warned about being a cultural Christian, being so caught up in the excitement of tagging along with the religious crowd that you rarely walk with or pursue him (Luke 14: 25-27). Choosing close friends who have integrity is different than walking with the religious crowd. Your ability and desire to have a godly inner circle is purely the result of walking with God first. When you make a choice each day to listen to Him, your heart will desire healthy friendships, and you'll know where you stand and how best to approach others who do not know Him.

When Shadrach, Meshach, and Abednego decided to stand firm in their faith, they caused a king and a nation to look higher. It's no surprise that these three were friends with Daniel. Remember the pace he set at the beginning of their academic program? Not only were they in school together, but they shared an understanding of reality. The same God-centered perspective. As a team, these friends had uncommon strength. When asked to turn their back on their trust in God, together they made this classic stand:

> O Nebuchadnezzar, we do not need to defend ourselves before you in this matter. If we are thrown into the blazing furnace, the God we serve is able to save us from it, and he will rescue us from

your hand, O king. But even if he does not, we want you to know,
O king, that we will not serve your gods or worship the image of
gold you have set up (Daniel 3:16-18).

When taking heat for keeping a pure heart, and when facing the
furnace of criticism for not compromising, God Himself defended
these friends. By standing together they invited the power of
God into their circumstances. They excelled in learning and in
life because their hearts were right. Together they changed their
campus and community.

Ask God to bring you the right friends during college, students
who are like-minded and live with integrity. Your peers can help you
develop your mind; they are not just a source for social skills development. Not only will they help you know what to think about, but
they can help you learn how to think. They can teach you new ways
of problem solving, new ways to make decisions. If you want to
gain insight, determine to be around friends who have insight. This
doesn't mean that you give up on those who do not know God or
who don't care about living His best for their lives. Some relationships you will have to break. God will want you to approach others
with a heart of ministry.

Advisors

George Ritzer in *Irrationality of Rationality* states, "…rational
systems inevitably spawn irrational consequences. Another way
of saying this is that rational systems serve to deny human reason;
rational systems are often unreasonable."[2] Within logical systems,
illogical consequences can and do arise. In much the same way that
new antibodies draw out the growth of new viruses, our seemingly
logical choices can have irrational consequences. We study, work,
and live in fallen systems. So, our decisions can have—often unknown
to us—unreasonable and counterproductive consequences.

God's plan for helping us make effective decisions in a fallen
world includes seeking out sound advice (Proverbs 19:20). Advice

can help us accomplish His best because it keeps us realistic and utilizes insight from multiple angles. Since life is not typically what it seems, good advisors keep us practical about ourselves and our goals as we continue to grow. If we will choose not to pretend, not to act from hollow social scripts, and instead seek outside perspective about our blind spots, we'll be able to make excellent decisions.

Richard Light (2001) in *Making the Most of College* says "Good advising may be the single most underestimated characteristic of a successful college experience..."[3] Applying sound advice can save you time and wasted energy during college. Searching out these perspectives will have positive, long-term benefits for you and others.

When you seek academic advice, you will have a better idea of how to complete your academic plan. You'll learn how to avoid debt when you ask someone who understands God's desire for finances. You'll avoid harmful relationships and develop new strength when you use wise counsel. Don't limit yourself to one mentor or advisor, but take the time to actively listen to multiple advisors and search out wisdom's perspective.

The best approach to working within a system of irrational consequences is to realize that we cannot trust ourselves; our hearts and minds are the most deceptive things in the world. Our decisions, which always have a spiritual and moral dimension to them, are best made when "in step with the Spirit" (Galatians 5:25). When we rely on the Counselor, we rely on His perfect mind, and the rippling consequences will have the best effect.

Parents

If you're like a lot of Christian students, one of your goals during college is to become responsible for yourself while developing a strong relationship with your family. To make this work, some of you will have to make a break from your high school selves and begin to approach your parents in a new, adult way. With this approach, your parents can prove to be a tremendous source of wisdom for you during college.

Ravi Zacharias in *I, Isaac, Take Thee, Rebekah: Moving from Romance to Lasting Love* teaches us the biblical importance of having our godly parents offer us their insight when choosing a spouse.[4] God gave us our parents for a reason, and college is definitely not a time to turn our back on them. Instead, it's a time to grow up and approach them in a new way.

We can honor our parents by sharing with them our unique experiences and what we are learning. We don't have to wait for them to initiate conversation or to ask the questions; instead, we can take the first step in developing new communication patterns and relationship boundaries with our families.

If you want to make the most of college, continue to honor your parents. Be patient with them as they adjust to you being in college. Work on your relationship with them. Be watchful about using them as a crutch for your decisions or over-relying on them for help. Instead, learn to ask them questions and to incorporate their insight into your decision-making. Pray for them as they adjust to your new family dynamics, and ask them to pray that you would know your purpose during college.

Romance

I like what Drs. Les and Leslie Parrot say about the importance of knowing who we are in order to have better relationships: "If you try to find closeness with another person before achieving a sense of identity on your own, all your relationships become an attempt to complete yourself."[5] This compulsion for completion, as they describe it, can cause us to miss out on our best relationships because we get stuck in a cycle of trying to figure out who we are by pursuing the wrong relationships. In our confusion, we end up chasing down the wrong people or over pursuing the right people.

When we know who we are in God, though, we know what closeness means with another person. We know which relationships to pursue because we're listening to Him. When we try the spiritual perspective of romance, we know why we are interested in romance, who we are, and where we are going in life. We're then able to discern our limits and avoid compromising. To have this freedom means that you listen to wisdom, rather than the world or your own assumptions about yourself. That wisdom guides your thoughts about who you are. It directs relationship timing. And it establishes healthy boundaries.

A spiritual perspective of romance keeps us realistic about waiting and when to go forward with a relationship. True spiritual romance is about dreaming God's best for our relationships. Eric and Leslie Ludy, authors of *When God Writes Your Love Story*, say:

> Little kids know how to dream. But as we grow up we quickly learn to be careful not to put too much stock in "happily ever after" conclusions. Once upon a time we innocently believed in fairy tale endings to difficult lives. But as we mature, and gain sophistication, we often stop believing in the Heaven at the end of the race, and so strangely dare only to believe in the hell in which we're struggling through today.
>
> As one of my disillusioned and forlorn friends in college once said, "Hell seems very appealing right now, compared to what I have to look forward to in this life." When we experience disappointment we quickly run to the nearest rationalization to purchase a protective armor, so as to never let disappointment hurt us again. We stop living for something beautiful, and start accepting something mediocre.
>
> In romance, we stop living for the "ride off into the sunset" endings, and start settling for "jerks-that-are-interested-in-only-one-thing" and flirts that only "want to feel special for a night."[6]

When we allow God to write our story, then our emotions don't dupe us into developing or continuing a relationship that is dangerous to our well-being. Choosing to live with Him each moment is much more important than the temporary pain or enticement we feel in other relationships.

Even though singleness may not be the dream of some, it is an opportunity to pursue God above everyone else, especially in a culture that is so hostile to waiting for true romance. Dr. Richard Land says, "You know, it is amazing to me, we have such a difficulty as Christians historically getting this right…in getting a proper balance in terms of understanding that both celibacy and the marital estate are equally spiritual and holy estates, depending on how you are living in them."[7] When you have been given a true sense of identity, then you can learn to live content in your relationship with your Creator no matter where you are in life. Singleness, even if just for a season, can prove to be the best means for your own pursuit of God.

Developing friendships with the opposite sex during college can teach you about yourself and can clarify in your heart the person that you are looking for in a spouse, but to have this freedom means that you continually give your motive over to your Guide so you can follow His lead. When you've spent time with God, seeking His guidance on romance and how best to honor Him with this type of relationship, you'll live with relational purpose. The closeness that you'll experience with others will only serve to help make you and your date become better people. You'll see that He is teaching you both about His best for relationships. Single or in a relationship, romance will always be about the realistic, sacred pursuit of God.

Faculty and Staff

As a student, it is your spiritual responsibility to develop a good working relationship with faculty and staff on your campus and to do your best as a student. Our instructions are clear, "work at it with all your heart, as working for the Lord..." (Colossians 3:23). We are to do our best work on assignments because of the Source of our motivation. When given specific guidelines to follow, follow them within the confines of conscience. When given beneficial advice, consider it.

Learn from your professors, but be balanced with your approach to them. We are to submit to those in authority but to hold our ground in truth. Before you become awestruck by some professor with lofty ideas and empty philosophy, consider 1 Corinthians 1:

> For the message of the cross is foolishness to those who are perishing, but to us who are being saved it is the power of God. For it is written: 'I will destroy the wisdom of the wise; the intelligence of the intelligent I will frustrate.' Where is the wise man?

> Where is the scholar? Where is the philosopher of this age? Has not God made foolish the wisdom of the world? For since in the wisdom of God the world through its wisdom did not know him, God was pleased through the foolishness of what was preached to save those who believe. Jews demand miraculous signs and Greeks look for wisdom, but we preach Christ crucified: a stumbling block to Jews and foolishness to Gentiles, but to those whom God has called, both Jews and Greeks, Christ the power of God and the wisdom of God. For the foolishness of God is wiser than man's wisdom, and the weakness of God is stronger than man's strength (1 Cor. 1:18-25).

It's no surprise that the college atmosphere is often the most antagonistic toward Jesus; His God-claim sounds foolish to many who create our curriculum and teach our courses. The intellects of this age encourage students to look no further than self or society or nature for truth because they choose not to see the reality of the Creator. They do not realize that His ways are higher and infinitely wiser because they don't know Him.

When you are searching for answers to tough questions during college, search out what God has to say. If you don't, you will be left with dozens of questions and no answers. You shouldn't get caught up in worthless arguments with professors, but you should get caught up in sharing truth in smart ways. I had a World Literature instructor who made it clear to our class that he was not a Christian. Knowing this, Kyle, a student sitting next to me, made it a point to write compelling papers in which he made exceptional arguments for God. I stopped by our instructor's office once to talk with him; he had invited the class to swing by and discuss the readings for extra credit. In the middle of our conversation, I asked him if he had read C.S. Lewis's *Mere Christianity* and what he thought about the book.[8] He said it was an interesting read and that he had always aligned himself most closely with Christian teachings. Then he said that just recently, because of one particular student's papers, he was becoming more convinced of Christianity and of God. I was glad to be in that class and to see the power of one student's papers in helping a half-convinced instructor understand truth.

Follow Kyle's lead. Know that God has placed you in the courses you are taking and around certain professors for a reason. Know that your topics and how you organize your presentations and papers are important. Approach your coursework with diligence and with an insightful heart. Faculty and staff can be some of the most influential people in our lives. They enjoy the college atmosphere and being around students. They like sharing ideas and learning new things, so come with a teachable heart; remember, though, who is guiding you and where to turn for answers.

If you have a hard time developing a servant-style leadership now as a student, what makes you think you will be a great employee in the future? Or an excellent boss? If you will work at servant-leadership now, then you will go to new levels of learning and influence during and after college. You will live up to your potential as a student.

Our Best Relationships

Your best relationships during college will build you up. They will make you a better person: "As iron sharpens iron, so one man sharpens another" (Proverbs 27:17). If you want exponential effects with your life, then be in the right relationships and be the right friend to others.

Be the kind of person who sets the pace. The kind of friend who lives above pressure and calls others higher. The kind of son or daughter who honors imperfect parents. The date who lives his true identity, has a biblical view of romance, and protects his heart by living good boundaries with accountability. The kind of student who inspires professors and staff. The child who enjoys relationship with God above all else.

try Iron Relationships

1. Get a mentor during college, someone who can show you how to grow, how to develop new ways of thinking and behaving, and how to discover your talents. If you pay attention, you

will have a handful of speakers, writers, and friends who can challenge you to go higher. Whom are you learning from?

2. Ask your parents to pray for you, that you will know what your purpose is and that you'll learn how to live in healthy relationship with others.

3. Pray for your friends, family, professors, date, and the staff at your school. Pray that God would use you to encourage and challenge them to be their best. Ask Him to give you a teachable heart.

4. There may be dozens of great student organizations on your campus. Anything from Ducks Unlimited to Students Who Like Movies. Why not be adventurous and give one a try? Or why not start your own with some friends? I think it would be great to hear about more spiritual movements that got their start as campus organizations.

5. Be the kind of friend that you enjoy being around. Someone who lives with integrity, is open to accountability, enjoys relationship, and looks out for others.

Isolated or Inspired?

But I found out everybody's different—the same kind of different as me. We're all just regular folks walkin' down the road God done set in front of us.

—Denver Moore, *Same Kind of Different as Me*[1]

LIVING INSPIRED DURING COLLEGE involves knowing that you are not alone. It means remembering "that your Christian brothers and sisters all over the world are going through the same kind of suffering you are" (1 Peter 5:9, NLT). Someone else is transferring from a community college to a university. Someone else is having a hard time focusing. Another student is making her way across campus in a wheelchair. Someone else is facing the challenge of being a student-athlete. Another friend feels alone in his faith.

Go beyond just thinking about yourself during college. Encourage those around you. God entrusts all of us with challenges so that we can recognize our continual need for Him and comfort others. Our experiences, no matter how difficult, have been uniquely tailored for us so we can demonstrate His work. If we humble ourselves, trusting Him fully, these challenges will stir up within us a desire to overcome. They'll cause us to look higher and to live inspired.

Community College Students

Community colleges are powerhouses when it comes to higher education. For instance, Florida Community College in Jacksonville has five campuses and more than 64,000 students.[2] The open-door policy of community colleges has propelled millions of college hopefuls into success. Take a look at this list of just a few of the accomplished individuals who got their start at two-year colleges:

- Gwendolyn Brooks, *Pulitzer prize-winning poet*
- Eileen Collins, *National Aeronautics and Space Administration (NASA) astronaut*
- Joyce Luther Kennard, *California Supreme Court justice*
- Jeanne Kirkpatrick, *former United Nations (UN) ambassador*
- Jim Lehrer, *news anchor*
- Robert Moses, *choreographer and dance company founder*
- Sam Shepard, *Pulitzer prize-winning playwright*
- James Sinegal, *CEO of Costco*
- Maxwell Taylor, *former chairman of the Joint Chiefs of Staff*[3]

As a community college student, you have just as much potential as anyone. I had a professor, a former Vice Chancellor of Students, who said that access to information, not necessarily where you go, is what matters most when it comes to college and learning. As a former community college student myself, I was glad to hear that. A community college student with the right motivation can do amazing things. We all know that Daniel "Rudy" Ruettiger overcame the odds to live his dream of playing college football, but we pass too quickly over the essential fact that it was his time at a junior college that made Notre Dame a reality.[4]

Tips...

1. Take the initiative to learn. Don't wait on someone else to get you motivated.
2. Know that community colleges and their students are vital to our communities, and to our nation.
3. Community colleges are first rate when it comes to student-centered teaching. You have just as much potential as anyone, so come through the open door with an appreciative heart and a motivated mind.
4. Community college faculty and staff are among the most caring educators. Thank them for their work, and learn from their lives.

First-generation College Students

Being the first in your family to attend college is tough. Unlike other students who have heard stories from their parents or grandparents about college, you may be coming with less knowledge about what to expect. I heard Dr. Angela Williams share her experience as a first-generation college student. As a freshman, she didn't know what to expect about being in college. She made a D on her first exam and was crushed. She immediately called her mom and said, "Meet me at the bus stop, I'm coming home." Her mom listened to her and promptly responded, "You're not coming home. You need to go talk with that professor." Thanks to her mom's advice, she went and talked with the professor who then realized that a mistake had been made when reporting the grade. For her, she needed help knowing how to navigate the college environment. She needed to see the importance of talking with her professors. She needed to know that she had what it took to succeed in college.*

First-generation college students often feel more anxiety with being in college because the experience is entirely new for them and their family. They're just not quite sure what to expect. If college is the dream that has been placed within your heart, then you are here for a reason. Live with the motivation to see your dream become a reality, and know that God will help you. There's nothing keeping you from being like millions of other first-generation college students who can and do succeed during college.

Be confident in knowing that God brought you here because He has a plan for your life, and He can use college to help you realize that plan. Take heart and know that He is here to help guide you in every new experience. Let Him use a TRIO program or an academic support office to show you how to navigate your campus or to teach you how to enhance your ability to learn. Find some friends to lean on and who can lean on you. Get to know your professors, and ask

---

*Information used with the permission of Angela Seawood Williams.

them for tips on being successful in their courses. Ask questions and learn how college works.

Tips...

1. Know that finishing college will mean big things for future generations in your family. I once talked with a community college student who wanted to challenge himself with college so he could inspire his kids to do the same with their lives someday.
2. Seek advice. Make time to go to a learning center or to get help with assignments. If you're taking prep courses, do your best to get a good foundation.
3. Get beyond feeling left out; don't wait for someone else to take the first step. Get involved the best way you know how by connecting with your teachers and your campus. Take a first year experience course.
4. Learn about the potential social and economic benefits of going to college.
5. Keep your soul fueled. Encourage yourself by knowing that God has a plan for your being here.

Lesbian, Gay, Bisexual and Transgender Students (LGBT)

I heard a professor share his testimony about struggling with a homosexual identity during college. Convinced that being gay was his fixed identity, he lived out the beliefs and behaviors that accompany this identity. During college, he came to a critical decision regarding who he was; he knew within his spirit that he was not living his best.

He decided that if this truly was his identity, then he would find confirmation from God. So he poured through Scripture, reading every passage he could find about identity and sexuality. He found no support for this identity, or his feelings, so he knew that it was time to rely on God as his identity source.

Professor Hough came to an understanding that the fall had affected all of nature and that his sexual orientation had been skewed from what God had intended. Now, he could stand with power in the presence of temptation and a sexual orientation that had been all he had known. As he looked higher, he could choose behavior that defied his impulse but was glorifying to God and in line with His original intent for his sexuality.

One of my favorite parts of his testimony was the support that he received from his friends at the BSU (Baptist Student Union) when he let them in on this part of his life. He experienced the healing that any of us receive when others gather to support us, when they encourage us with their words and actions and shelter us from the critical hearts of those who question whether or not change and growth is possible. He ended his testimony with an inspiring call for Christians, who do not struggle with homosexual desires, to lead the way in bringing encouragement and hope to those who do.*

LGBT students often experience intense isolation and personal pain during college. In fact, studies show that LGBT youth are at risk for suicidal behaviors related to their sexual orientation and identity.[5] Beyond the controversy of being LGBT and the reality that many of these students don't consider their attractions as unwanted, rests the reality of a need for compassion.

When confronted with a woman not living her best with her sexuality, Jesus took an unusual approach. Everyone else saw two choices: condemn her or let her off the hook (which would mean that he did not stand for truth). Jesus saw her need, and He chose compassion. Compassion amidst judgmental hearts exposed sin but revealed His grace. He chose mercy while showing her which direction to take in order to live out her true identity. During college, follow Christ's leadership and defend truth by being a person of compassion. Don't neglect the reality of sexual sin and its consequences, but do understand the complexity of identity development and the need for representing truth in love.

---

*Story used with permission. For a more detailed explanation, or to hear his entire testimony, contact Professor Jason Hough at JHough@jbu.edu.

Tips...

1. If you are an LGBT student, know that God loves you and that He wants His best for you. He has allowed you to carry the weight of this struggle, in a culture confused about sexuality, to reveal His power as He molds you into His image. He has chosen you for this burden so that He can reveal His strength to the world by working in your life. Be willing to deny your own feelings and listen to Him about your identity.

2. Become a student of sexual identity development, and learn how you and others can develop a healthy sexuality. Learn from the experts at NARTH (National Association of Research and Therapy of Homosexuality), and see what they have to say about unwanted homosexual attraction.[6]

3. Take the time to read Chad Thompson's testimony in, *Loving Homosexuals as Jesus Would*,[7] and visit www.Exodus.com for encouragement and help.[8]

From Home Education to College

Going from homeschool to college is a challenge, but it's not one you're facing alone. As the homeschool movement continues to grow into the millions, the number of homeschooled students attending college will only continue to increase. College, for these students, can represent a number of new, beneficial opportunities.

Home-educated students often exhibit a number of leadership qualities when entering college. The unique nature and flexibility of their individualized learning program can lend a favorable hand when adjusting to the self-motivated nature of college. Research has found that many homeschoolers are prepared for the academic rigors of college, scoring higher than the national average on the ACT.[9] Research has also shown that the "home-educated were certainly not isolated from social and group activities with other youth and adults. They were quite involved in youth group and other church activities, jobs, sports, summer camps, music lessons, and recitals."[10]

It is no surprise that many of these students adjust well to college and go on to be leaders. Some of our early national leaders were educated, at least in part, at home: Patrick Henry, William Penn,

Daniel Webster, Wilbur and Orville Wright, Abraham Lincoln, and Thomas Edison.[11] A nationwide study of home-educated adults even found that, "In essence, the home-educated were very positive about their homeschool experiences, actively involved in their local communities, keeping abreast of current affairs, highly civically engaged, going on to college at a higher rate than the national average, tolerant of others' expressing their viewpoint, religiously active, but wide ranging in their worldview beliefs, holding worldview beliefs similar to those of their parents, and largely home educating their own children."[12]

I know first-hand that home education can present many opportunities but that the transition to college can be a challenge. When is living your faith in this culture ever not a challenge? For those who are ready for the chance to grow, though, becoming a student who can relate to others in a learning community is a rewarding transition. The challenge for every student, despite level of preparedness, is to become an integrated, balanced adult.

Tips...

1. Be ready to address misconceptions associated with home education. Many students, staff, and professors are not familiar with homeschooling. Ask God to show you how best to assimilate into your new educational environment.
2. Many students are so nervous about messing up that they don't take the right risk with friends and opportunities. Listen to God about taking risks. Grow by learning about your unique campus culture and the other students.
3. Be ready for social pressure; it will come at you in a heightened way during college. God has said that He will guide you, so realize your need for Him in your relationships and with learning.
4. Be careful about a judgmental attitude. I watched a student completely sabotage herself as she struggled to work in a team. It didn't take long to see that her beliefs overshadowed her willingness to approach others with a caring heart. She got so caught up in showing others what her convictions were that she missed out on the opportunity of learning from and reaching out to the other students. She didn't know how to accommodate others

for the purpose of pulling them into her worldview. Instead, she approached them as though they were unreachable.

5. As you meet new people and learn their stories, don't compare yourself with them by focusing on things that you missed out on during your schooling, but instead focus on the opportunities that you did have. God has plans to use your experiences, even if they're lacking and you aren't prepared, to bring about His best.

Honors Students

As an honors student, you have some great opportunities in front of you. Not only are many of the courses that you're taking designed to motivate you to think at your best, but you may also have access to campus, travel, and scholarship opportunities not available to others. If you continue using your strong work ethic, desire to learn, and ability, you'll be able to make the most of these opportunities.

Do your best. Waste no time comparing yourself with others or being intimidated by their achievements. Run your own race. Fully engage your mind, but keep your thoughts based in reality. David, who possessed an exceptional mind and motivated personality, said, "My heart is not proud, O Lord, my eyes are not haughty; I do not concern myself with great matters or things too wonderful for me. But I have stilled and quieted my soul".[13] David, a king, a writer, a musician, and a brilliant leader, had learned not to think too highly of himself or to compare himself with others. Instead, he quieted his soul before God.

You have been given your talent and drive to use for helping. Don't get distracted by a system that won't deliver in the end. As an honors student, you have a unique responsibility to yourself. Don't limit your potential by getting trapped in the system of self-importance and constant comparison which academia all too often encourages.

Share your skills with other students. Learn to inspire and motivate others to pursue their best. If you're good with time management, make yourself available to help a friend or student who's not so great at it. If you have immense motivation, make it contagious. If academics come natural to you, then just remember that you're at a greater risk of being tempted to forget who gave you that ability. If you'll always make it a point to remember, then you'll go further than your plans will take you.

Tips...

1. Remember who gave you your ability and you'll avoid getting wrapped up in the empty side of academics.
2. See honors studies as an opportunity to enhance yourself so that you can help others.
3. Be careful about isolating yourself during your studies. Make time for friends and family.
4. You will accomplish more if you'll ask God to deal with your perfectionism. In fact, those with perfectionist tendencies are often less productive with their course work than those who simply do their best and are willing to take risks with the time they've been given.
5. If you struggle with overachievement, reevaluate what true success is. Be able to take a step back, look at each day, and relax knowing that you did your best.

Nontraditional Students

Traditional students are those students who begin college right after high school. If this is you, you're probably enrolled full-time and college is your primary focus with maybe a part-time job on the side. If you're a nontraditional student, your path has been a different. You may have one or more of these characteristics:

- Delays enrollment (does not enter postsecondary education in the same calendar year that he or she finished high school);
- Attends part-time for at least part of the academic year;

- Works full-time (35 hours or more per week) while enrolled;
- Is considered financially independent for purposes determining eligibility for financial aid;
- Has dependents other than a spouse (usually children but sometimes others);
- Is a single parent (either not married or married but separated and has dependents); or
- Does not have a high school diploma (completed high school with a GED or other high school completion certificate or did not finish high school).[14]

As a nontraditional student, you've had some life experiences. Maybe you've been in the military, have been working full time or have taken a break to spend more time with your children. Or maybe you don't have a high school diploma. Today, being nontraditional encompasses much more than just not going to college right after high school.

In fact, if you're a nontraditional student, then you're like a majority of today's college students. So, don't get intimidated. Don't doubt whether or not you're doing the right thing by being in college. If you're making some positive changes and you know this is where you're supposed to be, stop comparing yourself with other students. Know that there are a lot of students with similar background experiences. Keep doing your best.

Dr. Laura Rendon says that, "Even the most non-traditional students can be transformed into powerful learners through in- and out-of-class academic or interpersonal validation."[15] You have the potential to learn, so don't waste good energy worrying about whether or not you can handle the work load. Learn what it takes to succeed, and stay focused.

Tips...

1. You may not have as much time to get involved on-campus, but you can get to know your professors and the other students in your classes.

2. Don't hesitate to bring your practical life experience into the classroom. Other students will benefit from listening to your insight. Be careful not to come across as all-knowing or condescending, though; give others the freedom to be where they are in their own lives.

3. Confront feelings of inferiority with prayer; don't give them any room in your heart. It is because of Christ that we stand before others whole and with confidence in the person we are.

4. Be patient with professors, even if you're not fond of their teaching style. Learn to enjoy being in college.

5. Say no to anxious thoughts. Replace them by thinking about good things. Learn to overcome stress and to effectively manage your time.

Student Athletes

As a student athlete, you are in a place of influence. Campuses and communities are looking, often with a critical eye, at your response to your sport and to your education. Though the temptation may be there to take advantage of your privileges and influence or to neglect your education, being a true student athlete requires "balancing athletic and academic endeavors, balancing social activities with the isolations of athletic pursuits, balancing athletic success or lack of success with maintenance of mental equilibrium, balancing physical health and injuries with the need to keep playing, balancing the demands of various relationships."[16] This is a tough reality, but God wants to help you succeed by becoming a person of balance.

Being an athlete and doing your best in college is one of the most challenging roles a student can have. You're spending tireless hours working at your sport, which is why research shows that you could have a hard time developing an identity separate from your athletic identity.[17] Success at your sport and in your education will require realistic soul searching and a commitment to listening to

God about your priorities. Knowing who you are and where you're going is a must.

If you have been given ability for a sport and you want to gain a college education, then you'll have to do what it takes to succeed. A former student-athlete once told me that most college coaches know the importance of education; many of them have master's degrees, and some have doctorates. Completing your degree will require the same commitment that you use to excel in your sport. The same kind of determination that Brandon Burlsworth, a walk-on offensive lineman for the Arkansas Razorbacks football team, used to set himself apart in the details of his life. As a student, earning a bachelors and masters degree, and an All-American athlete, his legacy and devotion to God continue to call others higher even in his physical absence.[18]

If you want to receive the victor's crown, like Brandon has, then live to please God. Agree with Eric Liddell, from the movie *Chariots of Fire*, "I believe God made me for a purpose, but he also made me fast. And when I run I feel his pleasure."[19]

Tips...

1. Remember who your audience is. In reality, you are competing in a tournament with only one judge weighing in on your performance.

2. Analyze your motive for playing sports; know who you are now, during, and after college.

3. Seek out support for time management, personal accountability, and academics.

4. Use your same victory-driven thoughts and behaviors in the classroom and in your relationships.

5. For an inspiring look into Brandon's life, visit brandon-burlsworth.org or read Jeff Kinley's *Through the Eyes of a Champion*.[20]

Students with Disabilities

My disability is one piece of the picture—NOT the most important piece. I am a student, a sister, an aunt, a daughter, a Christian, and a country music fan. My disability is way down on my list of what is important about me. I don't want people to refer to me as 'that girl in the chair' or 'the person with the spinal injury,' but rather a person who is interested in languages that she won't stop learning…

—A college student[21]

I like this student's perspective. Her words challenge us to see the dimension in her life and her purpose during college. She encourages others to see the whole picture of who she is. Her determination is to be her best during college, to continue learning languages, and to change the hearts and perspectives of others.

It's empowering to be around individuals who inspire us to "go to the rock higher than I" (Psalm 61:2). Those who remind us that God is in complete control of our lives and our experiences. Sometimes the most influential lives are those that carry the burden of incredible personal challenges. They're often the most passionate and transforming individuals. Leadership expert John Maxwell adds, "A study of three hundred highly successful people, people like Franklin Delano Roosevelt, Helen Keller, Winston Churchill, Albert Schweitzer, Mahatma Gandhi, and Albert Einstein, reveals that one-fourth had handicaps, such as blindness, deafness, or crippled limbs. Three-fourths had either been born in poverty or come from broken homes, or at least come from exceedingly tense or disturbed situations."[22]

Individuals like Nick Vujicic, who was born without arms and legs, have seemingly impossible challenges before them. But they are the ones who cultivate the most vivid perspectives and lead with a passion that few experience. Leaders like Nick choose daily to see beyond the present challenge to the reality of their spiritual opportunity, often pushing the limits of vision into eternity. He knows that his life is meant to display the life of God and to focus on the gifts he has been given in Christ (John 9:3). He says that "we can't and we should not compare suffering," but instead we should each take up our own cross daily and focus on living as a family in God.[23] He has determined to have a higher mindset, and he inspires others to do the same.

Bringing encouragement and grace to others starts by seeing the depth of what God has entrusted us with. Perhaps, in spite of the extreme difficulties you face, you can be like Gianna Jessen who says, "I am so thankful for my Cerebral Palsy. It allows me to really depend on Jesus for everything."[24]

Tips...

1. Challenge yourself to stay positive, and to maintain your perspective by knowing who is in control of your life.
2. Don't let a lack of support or poor accommodations get you down. Take action when necessary, but stay focused on the passion God has placed within your heart to pursue your studies. Whether you're interested in languages or history or business, don't stop learning. Let God open your mind to what He has for you.
3. Get familiar with your college before you start. Take a course at your new school during the summer before your freshman year. Or take a freshman seminar course to learn about the campus and its support offices and to pick up study and time management skills.
4. Take the initiative for your college experience. Get to know others on campus, people you can encourage and be encouraged by.

Student Diversity

There is a growing body of research on the diversity of students and their experiences during college. A large part of this research has focused on African American and Hispanic students. More researchers are now looking at the college experiences of "American Indians, Asians, Pacific Islanders, Filipinos, Puerto Ricans, Cubans, and immigrant students from Asia and Central and South

America."[25] Researchers and higher education professionals want to understand your unique experiences so they can know how best to help you succeed. In fact, there are a number of programs and offices on campuses whose primary goal is to help underrepresented and international students achieve their goals and earn their degrees.

Minority students face a number of challenges with completing a college degree. Many students have to overcome poverty, family and cultural pressures, and weak academic preparation in order to assimilate into a campus culture. While we all face personal challenges during college, underrepresented and international students often add a number of complex, sometimes hidden, social and psychological hurdles when pursuing a degree.

For underrepresented students, overcoming personal and social challenges is certainly not easy. But it is definitely something that can be done with the right perspective and support. For instance, we know that, "Quality interaction with faculty seems to be more important than any other single college factor in determining minority student persistence."[26] We also know that, when students are given the right tools (*e.g.*, a positive outlook, language skills, time management skills, problem-solving skills, and communication strategies), they go further.

Student diversity is not limited to factors of culture and race. It also includes differences in our personalities and communication styles. Many times, it's our personalities that cause friction in our college relationships. As you continue to learn and appreciate diversity on your campus, learn about yourself and the temperaments of others. Also, keep in mind that if you want support and tools for success, be proactive and look in the right place.

Tips...

1. If you're a freshman, get involved in a first-year experience program. Check into a summer bridge program if you haven't started college yet.

2. Don't let yourself get in the way of God's best during college. Do your part to overcome social, communication, personality, and mental barriers.
3. Continue to talk with your academic counselor about your plans and goals, and seek out support from your Learning Center.
4. Take advantage of the summer to prepare for each upcoming year.
5. Communicate with your family about your experiences. They likely want to be involved in your college experience but might not know how to ask.

Social Sororities and Fraternities

Along with college athletics, sororities and fraternities are among the most debatable college topics. While service, professional, and honor societies fall beneath the umbrella of Greek organizations, it's the social fraternities and sororities that most often denote negative student behavior. Although originally founded on the principles of "justice, honor, truth, loyalty, love of wisdom, brotherly love, and unselfish service," these are not typically the first descriptions that come to mind when we hear the words *Greek life*.[27]

What is needed to bring out the best in Greek organizations? A return to the core principles on which they were founded. If these principles were lived out in the details of students' lives, then positive change would without doubt take place. Concerning fraternities, Baier and Whipple add:

> Perhaps one reason fraternities have come under so much negative scrutiny is that in addition to the discipline problems, legal liabilities, injuries, and deaths caused by fraternity hazing, sexual assaults, racism, poor scholarship, and alcohol and substance abuse, educators have been unable to find any evidence that fraternities contribute to the positive moral, ethical, and intellectual development of their members... The challenge to student affairs administrators appears to be clear. We must either find ways to redirect the values systems of

the fraternities on our campuses or we should commence
the process of eliminating this dinosaur from our midst.[28]

If fraternities and sororities are to contribute to the overall well-
being of our campuses, then these students must hold to construc-
tive values. Perhaps these changes will start with you, but make
sure that you're called to the task before you go trudging into battle.

The social connection that is promoted in the Greek system
can lead to groupthink, the tendency to think alike without questioning the motive or outcome of an action. This group mentality
and behavior is easily identified in binge drinking and hazing. Even
more unnerving, but certainly not surprising because of groupthink,
is the research that illustrates lower levels of identity and intellectual development among some Greek students, mainly those within
their first year of college.[29] If Greek life is for you, then know what
you're getting yourself into. Search out the right kinds of friends
within your organizations, and listen to God about your identity.

If you choose to live within this student culture during college,
and you know that you have been given this freedom by God, then
your guidelines are clear: "Religion that God our Father accepts as
pure and faultless is this…to keep oneself from being polluted by
the world" (James 1:26). Your mission during college is no different
from any other mission you'll have in life; it's to please God.

Tips…

1. Ask God what He thinks about your being in a Greek organi-
    zation. Listen to what He says, and handle the decision with
    prayer and fasting.
2. Conform only to God. I met a man once when I was working
    for the Salvation Army during college; he was homeless, an
    alcoholic, and had been in and out of prison. He, like several
    other men I met there, had cultivated his addiction to alcohol
    and other negative behaviors during college. He described his
    fraternity years as the "best days of my life," days that eclipsed
    the next 20 years of his life.

3. Your best defense in college is to seek out the places that you know you should be in and stay there until God shows you differently.

Working Students

Today, a majority of college students work while going to college. In 2000, nearly 80% of undergraduates worked as compared to 40% in 1960.[30] In addition to this increase, students are also working more hours. According to researchers, 19- to 23-year-olds worked an average of 25 hours per week, and students 18 and younger worked about 23 hours per week.[31]

Working part-time during college can keep you focused and on track with your time, but it's important to weigh the pros and cons with your work load. I talked with a freshman who had decided to buy a new SUV during her second semester on-campus. I saw her the following semester, and she was working a lot of extra hours because she was tied to the hefty car payment. Instead of the freedom and status she thought her new car would provide, she now had to work weekends and miss out on more than she had hoped. She traded the freedom that comes from driving an older car for the status of having a new car. I'm not sure that she considered the far-reaching effects—and the missed opportunities—of her decision.

Working the right number of hours during college can be beneficial on many levels. For many students, working is not an option; it's a must. However, making sure you have the time and energy to study can pay large dividends in the end. College is a great place, but many students need to think about pushing on through so they can start using what they've learned in a full-time job. Others, those who must work, may need to consider taking fewer hours to successfully carry the weight of work. So be careful about your work load. Make sure your schedule gives you the freedom to stay balanced as a working student.

Tips...

1. Apply the principles you are learning in class to your work environment. If you're taking a psychology class, then become a student of relationships and behavior at work. If it fits, connect your work experience with classroom discussions. Don't just sit back and listen.

2. Instead of working off-campus, try looking for an on-campus job; this can have a number of benefits (*e.g.*, it can save you travel time and connect you to campus employees and other students).

3. If you're going to work a lot of hours, find an institution or a program that will complement your needs and lifestyle. Check with your institution about receiving internship or cooperative education credit for your work experience.

4. Develop relationships with students you can rely on for help and information. Swap e-mail addresses during the first week of class.

5. Simplify your life and your spending. Create a budget for yourself.

6. Take a class on time management, and for starters, read *First Things First* by Stephen Covey.[32]

try Beyond You

As a college student, it's important to know what you're up against. To know your challenges, your strengths, and weaknesses. But it's significant to recognize that other students are also being tested. Will you go further than just caring about yourself during college?

Learn about your campus and get to know those who are facing their own challenges. What can you do to encourage a first-generation college student? A student-athlete? A student with a disability? A community college student? An LGBT student? A nontraditional or working student? An international student? When you see beyond yourself, you'll live confident knowing that you have a purpose higher than self.

Chapter 15

Higher Confidence

Who gets better grades than the SATs predict? The optimist. And the pessimists get worse grades than their SATs predict.
—Martin Seligman, *Learned Optimism*[1]

NOW IS THE TIME to begin living up to your potential. Let the past stay where it is. Move forward, trusting God to work out all of your failures and disappointments for good.

In education, living up to the positive expectations others have for us is referred to as the "Pygmalion Effect." When someone, especially someone we admire, says or shows us that they believe in us, a remarkable process begins to take place inside of us. Even despite low ACT scores, like I had, higher expectations encourage us to strive further and move on. We begin to see ourselves in a new way, in the positive way that they see us. They see our future as hope-filled, and we begin to see it that way too.

Teddy Stallard became a Pygmalion student. Unattractive and unmotivated, Teddy's records revealed a student who was in desperate need of encouragement: 1st grade showed promise but also a poor home situation, 2nd grade was okay but uncovered an ill mother and a negligent home life, 3rd grade was the year Teddy's mother died, and 4th grade found him slow and serious with a disinterested father. Despite knowing his story, his teacher Miss Thompson had a hard time loving Teddy as she did her other, more promising students. The turning point for Miss Thompson came, however, when Teddy brought her a Christmas gift. The other students laughed at the gaudy rhinestone bracelet with missing stones and the bottle of cheap perfume, but she immediately put them on, oohing and aahing. After all the students had gone home,

Teddy lingered at her desk to say, "I'm glad you like my presents, Miss Thompson... You smell just like my mother." After Teddy left, Miss Thompson fell to her knees and asked God to forgive her for her attitude toward Teddy. She realized she needed to become a person committed to helping and loving all of her students, especially the slow ones. As Miss Thompson began to see the potential in all of her students, and to help them each discover their unique strengths, Teddy began to dramatically improve at school. Miss Thompson had become an instrument of God in the classroom, and Teddy's life was changed for good. Years later, when Miss Thompson heard again from Teddy, it was a note that read:

> *Dear Miss Thompson:*
> *I wanted you to be the first to know. I will be graduating second in my class.*
> > *Love,*
> > *Teddy Stallard*

Four years later, another note came:

> *Dear Miss Thompson:*
> *They just told me I will be graduating first in my class. I wanted you to be the first to know. The university has not been easy, but I liked it.*
> > *Love,*
> > *Teddy Stallard*

And four years later:

> *Dear Miss Thompson:*
> *As of today, I am Theodore Stallard, MD. How about that? I wanted you to be the first to know. I am getting married next month, the 27th to be exact. I want you to come and sit where my mother would sit if she were alive. You are the only family I have now; Dad died last year.*
> > *Love,*
> > *Teddy Stallard*

Miss Thompson went to that wedding and sat where Teddy's mother would have sat. She deserved to sit there; she had done something for Teddy that he could never forget.[2]

What an inspiration. Because of Miss Thompson's kindness, Teddy experienced his potential in life. Because she believed in him and looked for the good, he found hope for his future. Teddy was called higher because of his teacher's ability to see into the depth of his life and to meet him where he was. She first lifted his heart with encouragement, and his mind followed with perspective.

Now is the best time to start seeing yourself the right way. God created you, like Teddy Stallard, with the capacity to learn and to be your best. He wants to use past failures and lost opportunities to shape you into a person of courage and depth. Sergei Rachmaninoff's magnificent piano concerto #2 lay just on the other side of his struggle with intense depression and the symphony that many critics considered an immense failure. God has given you a personality and talents that only you can offer to the world. So believe Him when He says He's come to give you an abundant life. If you will let your mind be filled with supernatural perspective, your desire to fully live will follow. When we take our focus off how much we think we love God and consider His love for us, we're transformed. You're not the same person that you were in high school; so use college as a time to allow the reality of God's love to recreate you.

Basing our expectations on what people think can have negative effects; it all depends on who our reference point is. If you're familiar with Cooley's "Looking Glass Self" theory, then you know why some students who binge drink during college often stop the behavior when they leave college. They know their boss doesn't expect them to binge drink, so they live up to the new expectations. During college, their behavior was motivated by what they thought their negative friends expected. Many students find themselves trapped in pornography because they feel it's just the norm, and because they feel that others just expect them to look at it the far reaching emotional, physical, relational, and spiritual consequences are completely ignored. Because we see ourselves through the eyes of our peer group, it's essential to be around the right perspectives.

It's no surprise that research supports the reality that positive thinkers exceed their ability in school, and pessimists drop below their potential.[3] God has given you potential. Again, believe Him. Do your best and think your best. How? By maintaining a vivid perspective during college. Learn to live up to His expectations for your life, His standard of excellence and worth, and your confidence will be based in reality because you'll see yourself and others in the right way.

When encouraging words are scarce and when you feel discouraged, know that He believes in you. You are created in His image, a reflection that He loves. You have the freedom to learn, so focus on the future He's bringing. Let the past be used as energy for overcoming future challenges.

try Spiritual Confidence

1. Live up to God's expectations for your life. You will go higher and your confidence will be real.
2. Be like Miss Thompson and genuinely believe in another student. Invest yourself in him with encouragement, and give him grace to grow during college.
3. Get around those who have high expectations for life, so you can be encouraged to take a step further. Professors who confront a limited perspective on potential. Mentors who ask the tough questions. Friends who have big dreams too. People you can draw strength from.
4. Even optimism can be learned and pessimism unlearned. Practice acting confident, even if you don't feel confident. As Joyce Meyer says, sometimes you just have to do things afraid.[4] The confidence will come afterward.
5. See yourself through the right eyes:
   a. "I am fearfully and wonderfully made" (Psalm 139:14, KJV).
   b. God gives me sound instruction (Proverbs 4:2, KJV).
   c. God will always guide me (Isaiah 58:11, KJV).
   d. I am called to learn to do right and to help others (Isaiah 1:17, KJV).

Chapter 16

Reference Point

The highest function of higher education is the teaching of things in perspective, toward the purpose of enriching the life of the individual, cultivating the free and inquiring mind, and advancing the effort to bring reason, justice, and humanity into the relations of men and nations.

—J. William Fulbright (1905-1995)[1]

IMAGINE YOURSELF WALKING ACROSS the stage at graduation, diploma in hand and smile on your face. What do you hope to have accomplished during college? To have gained? When you tell others about your college experience, what will you remember about the kind of person you were, the kind of life you lived?

Having vision of the good plans of God is fundamental to your success during college. It's what will keep you focused on your goals and keep you from wasting your time. From getting stuck or losing ground spiritually. It's what will keep you listening to Him. Oswald Chambers writes,

'Where there is no vision…' When once we lose sight of God, we begin to be reckless, we cast off certain restraints, we cast off praying, we cast off the vision of God in little things, and begin to act on our own initiative. If we are eating what we have out of our own hand, doing things on our own initiative without expecting God to come in, we are on the downward path, we have lost the vision. Is our attitude today an attitude that springs from our vision of God? Are we expecting God to do greater things than He has ever done? Is there a freshness and vigor in our spiritual outlook?[2]

As a college student, now is the best time to cultivate a spiritual perspective for your life. If higher education is about the teaching of things in perspective, then place your viewpoint within the realm of eternity. Don't wait until after graduation to create a vision for your life. Don't wait to take steps to see that vision become a reality. Let your motivation, the bridge between your vision and the reality of your future, keep you in a determined focus. Why wait to make a difference in others' lives when you can start this very moment with the people closest to you? Why wait to advance reason, justice, and humanity?

If you'll live listening to God and seeking perspective from those whose lives are vibrant, you'll go further than you would have ever imagined during college. Stop questioning how God is going to use your experiences, he's going to come through for you on the calling that He has placed within you because He has given you a future and a hope (Jeremiah 39:11).

My papa is a WWII veteran. Our family always enjoys being around him. His spiritual legacy enriches our lives. I still enjoy asking him questions about his experiences of courage as he stood for justice amidst the night of war. Once, after he'd finished telling me about the South Pacific, I asked him about his motivation; at 85 he works full-time as a building inspector in Texas. His drive and personal intensity are unrelenting.

He's always had an insatiable desire to learn, an amazing work ethic, a huge heart for family and for others, and more than anything a vivid perspective. I won't forget what he told me: "The war is my reference point. When we got back, it was time to move on, and we did." He moved on and up. He continues to draw a lifetime of positive motivation from the darkness of his reference point. For him, everything after the war was a privilege and an honor. I have never fought in a war, but I've used my grandpa's experiences as a reference point in my own life. Because of his life, I have the privilege and the freedom to succeed.

Want to increase your passion and drive? Change your perspective. If you need a reference point, listen to those whom God has placed in your life. My papa is not much for giving any space to negative thoughts in his mind, so you can imagine how refreshing he is to be around. I have a friend whose favorite quote by her grandpa, also a WWII veteran, was "Getting older ain't for sissies." Isn't that great?! If you're going to chase down life and live it to its fullest, then get the right perspective and do what it takes to press on.

Your determination to have an understanding heart is what will take you furthest during college. It's the students who are praised for their effort, instead of for being "really smart," that tackle more difficult tasks.[3] Why? Their perspective is different. They're more willing to take risks, more willing to pick themselves up and try again. Students like this are focused on the goal, not on themselves. Their vision and determination are persistent. They know they have what it takes to succeed, so it's just a matter of using their determination to see things through. Having a high IQ can be a good thing, but having the determination to maintain the right vision for your life is best.

I know a professor who dropped out of school in the 9th grade. After a decade, she decided to return to school. Now with Ph.D. in hand, she spends her time helping change the lives and perceptions of her students and community. She encourages students, especially those who come from poor families like herself, to know that they have what it takes to succeed. It doesn't take long for those she meets to feel her insightful perspective because she lives to help others.[4]

Live listening to God and you'll live to change lives. We'd all be better off if we would follow Warren Webster's advice: "If I had my life to live over again, I would live it to change the lives of people, because you have not changed anything until you've changed the lives of people."[5] Don't wish that you'd lived fully, spiritually: be the kind of person that you know you're destined to be. Expecting God to do great things and listening to Him in the details is the best kind of outlook for you and everyone you're around. There's nothing keeping you from living with a vivid spiritual perspective. A refreshing attitude will inspire those you're around, and help you see the significance in your four years.

Try Spiritual Perspective

1. What's your reference point for succeeding in college?
2. Whom has God placed in your life for you to draw strength and perspective from during college? Who will draw strength from your success stories some day?
3. Make time to read inspiring books and articles. Learn to experience life through someone else's eyes.
4. Students either progress or regress spiritually during college; there's not an in-between. What are you doing now to ensure that you're where you could be in four years? Don't wait until graduation to start practicing your vision for your future; start seeing God at work in your life now. Start asking Him to help you with your papers, your projects, and your relationships.
5. Travel can enhance our perspectives. Consider experiencing different cultures through a study abroad or mission trip during college.

Four Significant Years

RECENTLY, I TALKED WITH a freshman who came by to discuss his courses for the spring semester. I asked him about some of his transfer courses because his transcript didn't reflect the work he had completed. I told him that to be accurate with our discussion we would need a copy of his transfer work. Without hesitation, he started shifting through the stuff in his backpack. He pulled out the transcript from his previous school and said, "God reminded me to bring it this morning. I wondered why, and now I know."

This was intriguing considering he didn't know me. It was small but significant information at a public university where that language is atypical. Students who talk with God about the details of life during college have no trouble listening to him about their future. This student clearly knows "that a man's life is not his own; it is not for man to direct his steps" (Jeremiah 10:23). He is watching and listening as God directs his every step.

Practical Steps

Each year of college is just as significant as the next. Every semester there are steps you can take that will help you make the most of your time and life. After all, school is expensive. Not only are you and taxpayers (if you're at a public institution) paying money for you to be here, but a semester also costs you three and a half months of your life, which is a resource you can't get back. So make it worth the price, and see the significance in what you're doing.

Typically, during your 1st and 2nd year, you'll need a lot of information in order to make good decisions. You'll need to talk with advisors, read your catalog of studies, get to know your way around campus, get connected, explore your college website, and ask lots of questions. As you move into your junior and senior years, you will still need information, but having a mentor to guide you through your major courses, the graduation process, and into a career or professional or graduate school will be key to your success.

Take a look at some of these suggestions, but know that they are not comprehensive and are not limited to one year. A number of students finish earlier than four years, and some undergraduate programs are built around a five-year curriculum. Many of these are principles and skills that can help you each semester so establish relationships with academic, financial aid, scholarship, admissions, and career counselors who can help guide you through each transition and semester.

Freshman Year

Here's your first and most important step in college: determine to keep a clear conscience. As Daniel started his program, he "was determined not to defile himself..." (Daniel 1:8 NLT). While others were wasting their time with empty behavior and ideas, he was doing his best to live with integrity, and because of his choice he received "an unusual aptitude for understanding every aspect of literature and wisdom" along with "the special ability to interpret the meanings of visions and dreams" (1:17 NLT). Because of his excellent spirit, he received understanding, and he found favor with his leaders.

If you want to make the most of your freshman year and of college, keep a pure heart. When others are wasting their time with worthless behavior, stay focused on your purpose, and God will bless you with wisdom and the ability to make right decisions. So amidst the fast-paced, often confusing, moments of your first semester and year, determine to keep a clear conscience!

First-year Tips...

Your Mind

1. Set a positive, determined tone for all four years during your first year by developing the right thoughts: "I can do what God has called me to," "I have the ability to listen to God," "I have the strength that He provides," "My aim is to please God with all that I am."
2. Take ownership for your college experience. No one else can; you're in charge of you. Remind yourself of the opportunity and privilege before you to grow.
3. Ask God to help you change from a high-school to a college mentality. You're a different person now. Even your letters of recommendations from high-school teachers don't carry the weight they used to. Know your priorities.
4. Learn techniques to manage your time. Get a planner and learn how to keep a calendar.

Your Network

1. Ask God to show you where to get involved on campus. Ask Him to bring you iron relationships.
2. A few deep friendships are better than a lot of acquaintances. Be careful about over-committing as you work toward balance in relationships.
3. Ask God to help you in your relationship with your parents. Become a student who looks to them—as well as to other sources of wisdom—for counsel, not to solve your problems for you. Grow into an adult son or daughter who respects and honors your parents.
4. Get to know one or two of your professors or teaching assistants.
5. Learn how to navigate your campus, and learn important contact information. Where is the advising center? Where can you get help with papers or math homework? Who can you talk with about scholarships? Where's the library? Campus Police Department?

Your Body

1. Change your perspective of food. See it as important for maintaining a high level of energy so that you can do your best on your assignments and in class.
2. Right food can help you avoid making bad decisions (Isaiah 7:15).
3. Look for small ways to stay active. Take the stairs when you can, or ride your bike to class.
4. Get more sleep than most college students. Rest is what God has given our bodies. Don't miss the blessings of sleep. A little R and R brings health and a fresh energy for accomplishing the tasks.
5. Go to the campus fitness center several times a week, and ask a friend to go with you.
6. Honor God with your sexuality by keeping a clear conscience and by avoiding compromising situations.

Your Academics

1. Maintain a solid GPA. It's less stressful than trying to bring it back up in the future.
2. Success in most freshman courses depends on going to class, so go!
3. Learn your degree requirements.
4. Develop an educational plan. Map out your upcoming semesters so that you can have a mental picture of where you're heading.
5. Learn to be an active listener by developing good note-taking skills.
6. Figure out your learning style(s). Ask your advisor about taking a learning inventory.
7. Get to know your academic advisor, and go to your advising meetings with ideas. Take charge of your degree plan.
8. Create a master calendar of important dates, and keep it where you can see it (*i.e.*, registration, dropping or adding courses, projects, exams, finals).
9. Explore your major (contact your advisor or career center for tips on how to do this).

10. Take a first year experience course if you want to learn more about your campus and need a place to connect.
11. Take a balanced course load. Some students, depending on how academically prepared they are, start off by taking fewer classes (to build their skills and confidence) and add semester hours as they go.
12. Think ahead. Would you like to study abroad your junior year? Then why not start with some basic research now?
13. Get summer internship or work experience.

Your Spirit

1. Read a Proverb each morning; God's Spirit will remind you of words and phrases to think about throughout the day.
2. Write down a verse on a note card, keep it with you, and read it every chance you get.
3. Use your spiritual gifts, and ask God to protect you from yourself and your areas of weakness.
4. Get active spiritually. Find a group of friends with the same heart for good. Develop the habit of short, practical prayers throughout the day.
5. Help others with their experiences. Be an encourager.

Sophomore Year

Your second year is just as important as your first. Enjoy the comfort of feeling more connected with your college. But don't get too relaxed. There's work to do! Even if the newness and excitement is starting to cool, don't let your passion for being here and for finding your mission slow down. Stay focused on your goal of living right in the details.

When faced with new, complex decisions about your degree plan and future, handle them with wisdom. As you make smart choices, thank God for giving you a practical mind. Thank Him for giving you new insights, ways of thinking, and new opportunities.

Second-year Tips...

Your Mind

1. Learn how Jesus thinks. Read through the Gospels, noting His response and what He said to others.
2. Learn strategies for boosting your memory. Try mnemonic techniques or the Loci method. Read Dr. Minirth's *A Brilliant Mind* for some helpful strategies.[1]
3. Continue to work on your test-taking skills. Talk with someone from your Learning Center about techniques.
4. Be a part of a Bible-based discussion group, and have conversations about what God has shown you during the week.
5. If it fits with your plan, take an elective that sounds interesting to you.
6. Attend a guest lecture.
7. Start building your personal library.

Your Network

1. Get involved with an organization related to your major.
2. Search out relationships that encourage and promote integrity in your life.
3. Ask a friend or someone from your family to pray for you during the week, and pray for them.
4. Learn to balance your social schedule. One leadership role (*e.g.,* treasurer, vice president, president) can outweigh several organization memberships.
5. Work at connecting with your teaching assistants, advisors, and professors. Talk with them after class, or schedule a time to visit with them about your classes.
6. Stay connected with the godly voices in your life. Cultivate depth in your friendships.
7. If it fits with your schedule, make time to volunteer.

Your Body

1. Take a health class as an elective, or sign up for an aerobics class or intramural team.

2. Keep a journal of what you eat for a week to evaluate your food habits. Compare your notes with the food pyramid and adjust to reflect a balance.
3. Learn how your body responds to stress. Take a whole foods multivitamin and get some good advice about eating, breathing, and exercising to overcome stress. Read Dr. Colbert's book *The Bible Cure for Stress.*[2]
4. Avoid worthless and empty behavior.

Your Academics

1. Continue to see yourself as primarily responsible for your course work and your academic plan.
2. Learn the history, traditions, and mission of your campus.
3. Talk with your advisor and a career counselor about your future plans and goals.
4. Continue to explore your major.
5. Develop a plan for graduation.
6. If you're interested in graduate or professional school, talk with your advisor about prerequisite work.
7. Shadow someone who is in a career that interests you, and attend a workshop about career decision making.
8. Check with your department about scholarships for juniors and seniors that you can apply for in time for next year.

Your Spirit

1. Take a few minutes to reflect on your first year. What were your accomplishments? Failures? What did you purpose in your heart? Confess anything hidden, and ask God to help you leave the past where it is and to move into the promise of a new year.
2. Pursue excellence. Live a cut above the crowd.
3. Ask God to set the pace for your motivation.
4. Ask God to help you overcome anxiety; worrying just keeps us from being our best now.
5. Recognize the principle of sowing and reaping. What kinds of seeds are you planting now that will continue to grow during and after college?
6. Refresh your mind and heart by reading Scripture.

Junior Year

The seeds you have been sowing are growing. If you continue to plant the right seeds, you will set yourself up for great opportunities. Now is the time to "Sow your seed in the morning, and at evening let not your hands be idle, for you do not know which will succeed, whether this or that, or whether both will do equally well" (Ecclesiastes 11:6). Continue to branch out during your third year. Be deliberate with your decisions.

Researchers have found that for many juniors, "There is a sense of mastery, intellectual excitement, and academic purpose," and they "are also beginning to think more concretely about the future. They see themselves as having turned a corner and entered the downward (or outward bound) side of their college experience."[3] As you continue to master new material and grow, remember who brought you to this point. When Daniel was blessed with new insight, he exclaimed,

> Praise the name of God forever and ever, for he has all wisdom and power. He controls the course of world events; he removes kings and sets up other kings. He gives wisdom to the wise and knowledge to the scholars. He reveals deep and mysterious things and knows what lies hidden in darkness, though he is surrounded by light. I thank and praise you, God of my ancestors, for you have given me wisdom and strength. You have told me what we asked of you and revealed to us what the king demanded (Daniel 2:20–23, NLT).

Take your college experience to a higher level by thanking God for guiding you. Thank Him for blessing you with insight. Thank Him for the opportunities to practice what you're learning. Continue to do your best by living with integrity and by planting seeds of kindness and truth.

Third-year Tips...

Your Mind

1. Take a course that sounds challenging and interesting. Don't be afraid to venture into a course that will give you the opportunity to defend your faith. The experience just might stretch you and show you God's principles at work in a new way.
2. Read a book purely for enjoyment, not for class. Be willing to consider new authors and different genres than you may have in the past.
3. Keep a journal of your experiences, and look for God's hand in the details.
4. Do a crossword or Sudoku puzzle, dream about the future as you watch the clouds roll in, go for a quiet walk, or call your grandparents and let them know how college is going instead of spending your time on-line or watching TV.
5. Read through a classic Christian book with friends and meet to discuss the parts you've highlighted.
6. Pursue God with your entire mind.

Your Network

1. Provide leadership to a team, or help plan an event for a service group.
2. Sign up to be an ambassador on campus, or spend some time in conversation with a visiting international student.
3. Continue to work on your relationship with your family.
4. Talk with a faculty member from your department about your interests and plans for the future. Ask her about her research interests or why she chose her field of study.

Your Body

1. Write down some exercise goals for yourself.
2. Try some new ambitions: train for a marathon, learn a new sport, or just regularly spend time walking around campus.
3. Skim-read some books on health. Apply some new principles to your diet, exercise plan, or way of thinking. Consider Jordan Rubin's *The Maker's Diet* for a refreshing perspective.[4]

Your Academics

1. Visit with your professors, academic counselor, and a career counselor about career planning or graduate/professional school.
2. Explore careers related to your major. Talk with people about their careers, go to a career fair, and search the web.
3. Polish your interviewing skills. Do a mock interview with a friend or career counselor.
4. Get your resume ready.
5. Take your graduate or professional school entrance exam, and know the application deadlines for graduation and professional school.
6. Apply for internship opportunities.
7. Participate in service learning.
8. Review your degree requirements with your advisor, and plan your remaining courses for each semester of your senior year.

Your Spirit

1. Be genuinely concerned for others and support them in their successes and failures. Learn how to intercede for others in prayer.
2. Confront issues you're facing with in-depth Bible study (*e.g.*, read all you can on maintaining peace in your life).
3. Volunteer for activities that help you sharpen your spiritual leadership. Lead a Bible-based small group.
4. Plan a trip to an inspirational or leadership conference with some of your friends.

Senior Year

Making the most of college won't just happen; you'll have to keep the right attitude and take practical steps. Herant Katchadourian and John Boli, researchers at Stanford University say, "The key question in the freshman year is, What am I going to do in college? In the senior year it is, What am I going to do after college? In the freshman year one asks, Where are you from? In the senior year the question is, Where are you going next year?"[5]

As you transition from "what am I going to do in college" to "what am I going to do after college," remember that God has a unique purpose for you during your remaining semesters. Even though your life questions and concerns will change, God will not. He wants you to ask Him for advice about what steps to take and what kind of person you should be; He wants you to trust Him.

Fourth-year Tips...

Your Mind

1. Reflect on what God has taught you so far during college. What have you learned? What are your mental strengths? What does He want to accomplish in your mind this year?
2. Continue to learn His perspective for your field of study.
3. What problem solving strategies can you learn this year? What new methods for mastering the information in your major? What specialized language can you continue to learn?

Your Network

1. Talk with a career counselor about the process of applying for jobs or for professional or graduate school.
2. Learn how to effectively network for job opportunities.
3. Choose not to let envy enter your heart as you and your friends step out into new opportunities.
4. Be a mentor to an incoming freshman.

Your Body

1. Begin looking to buy professional work clothes. Have a nice suit to wear to interviews. (You don't have to spend a lot—check the sale racks during the off seasons, and mix and match with what you already have. Also consider second-hand shops.)
2. Remember again: Sleep for your body's health.
3. Eat healthy, whole foods so you can continue to do your best.

Your Academics

1. Know important senior year deadlines.

2. Apply for graduation, and make sure you have everything ready to go for graduating.
3. Apply for graduate or professional school.
4. Finish strong with your course work and your program.

Your Spirit

1. Protect your heart at all costs.
2. Remember who is in control and who gave you the opportunity to be in college and to learn.
3. Let patience have its way, no matter the cost, as you're guided to your next step.

Trust, Search, Wait, and Grow

I talked with a student once who was applying to a professional school. We were discussing steps he could take to improve his application and strategies for the admissions interview. We even did a mock interview. As we talked, I could tell he had a sense of destiny with his decision to go to the only school he had applied to. He seemed to know it was the career and school for him. He had applied himself, stayed active on campus, and sought advice from different staff and faculty at our school. After we finished talking, I made a comment about the importance of having a Plan B when applying to these types of programs. His response: "God's got my back on this one." I wasn't expecting that. I was surprised and inspired by it. God had given him a deep contentment about his decision. That was our last conversation on campus; he was accepted to the program.

Remember that your hard work will be rewarded in the way that God sees best and in His time. He has made hope plans for your future so trust Him during your transitions. He wants to prepare you for your next opportunity so humble yourself as you search, and wait for His move. When you let patience have its way, you'll grow into the kind of person that you were destined to be. You'll grow into the person who can handle the task that God is calling you to.

To succeed during college, there are important steps to take, but beyond these are qualities that you'll need to possess. As a student you only have two decisions: to recognize your spiritual journey and ask for help or to ignore your spirituality and miss out on God's best for your life. Make the most of every opportunity, and be the kind of person you were destined to be:

Try **Higher**	*Try* **Own Way**
Higher Thinking	College Thinking
Lead by Example	Follow by Pressure
Spiritually Active	Spiritually Passive
Wise Decisions	Empty Decisions
Spirit-Led Response	Impulsive
Pursue Maturity	Content with Immaturity
Seek Insightful Advice	Make Own Decisions
Humble	Self-Centered
Teachable	Already Know
Integrity Is Central	Fitting-in is Central

Your Purpose, God's Provision

A life lived listening to the decisive call of God is a life lived before one audience that trumps all others—the Audience of One.
—Os Guiness[1]

WHEN YOU ARE CALLED to a task, God will open the right doors for you. He'll provide you with the wisdom, motivation, and resources to complete the task. He'll do what it takes to point you in the right direction of a major and career field. He'll make sure you have what you need to fulfill your calling; just listen to Him.

Dad was unexpectedly laid off from his job as a salesman when I was 12. It was definitely tough and confusing on our young family. What the rest of us didn't realize was that Dad had known in his heart for a while that it was time for a change. Deep down, he wanted to be back in the classroom teaching art.

The week Dad lost his job he went to visit my grandmother in the next city over. As he was coming home, a couple that he knew recognized his car and waved at him to pull over. They asked about Mom and my brother and me. And then they asked him about his job. He explained that he had recently been laid off. They probed a little deeper and asked about his plans. He said he would like to teach, the career that he had started right out of college. They asked him what it would take for him to get started again. He told them he had talked with a local university and would need $600 dollars to take the teacher licensure courses.

They carefully listened to Dad tell his story, and, after he finished, they explained to him that they had been thinking about him lately, that God had placed him on their hearts. After that, they told him that they would like to pay for him to return to school. They pulled out their checkbook and wrote a check for the full amount.

At 44, my dad returned to college as a nontraditional student to pursue the career he loved. I'm not sure of the number of lives he's touched since then by teaching, but I know it's a lot. Last year, I read an article in the local paper about him titled, "Art Teacher Urges Students to Greatness." It said his students had entered the state's Congressional Art Competition for six years in a row and had placed first for five of those years. When asked about his success, he said, "I just do what I'm supposed to do, and the Lord takes care of the rest." He listened to his calling, was nudged in the right direction, and trusted God for the provision.

When God places a dream in your heart, He will cause it to become a reality. Nick Vujicic, of Life Without Limbs, tells the story of a young woman he met during his evangelistic tour. On Sunday while travelling to the other side of town for his sixth speaking engagement with a number of well-known Christian pastors and business leaders, his team decided to stop for lunch at a restaurant that was not on their initial agenda. Once in the restaurant, a waitress found herself breaking into uncontrollable sobbing as she turned to see Nick sitting in the restaurant where she worked. She began speaking hurriedly to Nick in her native language, so Nick pleaded with one of the pastors to translate what the woman was saying. Nick found out that six months ago the woman had become desperately depressed. Her family was extremely poor and she felt as though she was at the end of her rope. She didn't want to go on living. She didn't see the purpose of her life and she cried out to God asking to hear from Him. She ended up attending a church where they showed Nick's DVD. As she listened to Nick, she realized that God had a plan for her life. God also impressed on her heart that she was to start a children's ministry.

Nick writes, "Circumstantially, it was more than an impossible dream! At times have you been there too? When I entered that restaurant, she had been fasting and praying steadfastly toward that end for six months! She'd needed a job, and God had provided this restaurant work. But it had taken her eight hours away from home and family. Just to live, she had to work 10 hours a day, 7 days a week and was even living at the restaurant! She wondered how on earth she could even start a children's ministry without a degree. And truer still, how could she, impoverished as she was, even consider attending a Bible College, which was her desire? Admittance to Bible Colleges was difficult and incredibly expensive. She had no money and no time. Even so, *this was her dream, a seed that God had planted in her heart! And* now, here I show up in this restaurant where she works! She was simply overcome with emotion!"

As she told her story that day, Nick was not the only one listening. Unknown to the woman and to Nick were the roles of the men who sat at the lunch table. When the woman left the room, Nick began to discuss with the pastors and business leaders his intent to sponsor the young woman. As he continued, one pastor spoke up and said that he had condos available on the campus of his church and he would let her live in one if she went to Bible College. Another business leader spoke up and offered to sponsor the entire endeavor. As he and Nick discussed who was going to sponsor the young woman, a man on the opposite side of the table said, "I'm the President of the Bible College." That day, providentially, the young woman's impossible dream awoke in the realm of reality.[2]

God's provision comes in many different ways. College isn't for everyone, but if it's where you know you're supposed to be, then God will make a way for you. I knew college was for me but that massive school loans weren't. I had considered going to a private college, but the cost of tuition didn't fit with what my family and I could afford. For me, starting at a two-year college was the best financial fit. I may have had to live at home a bit longer, but graduating with a degree debt-free was worth it. When I got married during graduate school, I was also working full-time on campus. My wife and I chose to live in a 450-square-foot apartment on campus for two years, to give us the freedom to stay focused on school. It wasn't the most extravagant place to live with its cement floors and cinder block walls, but we did manage to graduate with no debt and save up $20,000 because of living there.

For my wife, making good grades during junior high and high school and applying for scholarships was how she allowed God to provide for her during college. I talked with a student once about preparing for graduate school, and as a college junior he had already saved up several hundred dollars just for the application fees of the three schools to which he wanted to apply. He was planning ahead, the same discipline he used as an incoming freshman. I have a friend whose dad knew he wanted to be an engineer, so he worked for four years to save up money before going to college. You don't hear about commitment like that too often!

God's provision involves making tough decisions and sticking with your principles. If you'll follow His lead, he'll show you how to live in financial freedom during college. Listen to what Dave Ramsey says about going to college:

I think there are two reasons to pursue an education.

1) If a degree in your chosen field will open doors to career opportunities. The truth is that in many fields a degree will not open doors. Consider whether all the costs balance against the financial rewards.

2) To improve your life quality through the pursuit of knowledge. If your reason is personal growth and to do what God has called you to, make sure you go slow and pay cash to avoid getting into trouble. Use wisdom for the sake of your family. Don't make your future hostage to student loans.[3]

God's provision includes giving you the ability to see into your future and to avoid making decisions that will keep you down. Don't settle for less during college; know that God will provide a way for you to accomplish what He has placed within you. God—the same God who equipped Joseph to lead a nation, who filled Solomon with wisdom, who gave Daniel focus, vision, and friends of integrity to fulfill his mission—wants to equip you in every way to fulfill the unique plan He has for your life.

try Trust

1. Will you risk trusting God for the best when it comes to providing for you? Why wouldn't He want to help you finish your program?
2. Don't try to figure out your finances on your own. You'll end up exhausted, and you'll miss out on what God is trying to teach you. Talk with your financial aid advisor, and scholarship office, use biblical principles, and seek wise counsel before taking out school loans and when planning for your finances during college.
3. If you'd like to work part-time and have the skills to balance this with school, check into jobs on campus or with your financial aid advisor about work study positions. You can also look for jobs near your campus that will be flexible with your schedule or for employers who offer tuition assistance for their employees.
4. Get creative about paying for college; you don't have to settle for debt. I saw a guy once on CNN who said, while he was brain-storming ideas to pay for college, he decided to start a website and sell space for a dollar a megapixel. Last I checked he was on his way to his first million.
5. Have a vision for your money, even if you don't have much. People who are trustworthy with a little can be trusted with much more. Learn to effectively manage and be content with what you have. See *Try Money Vision* for ideas on living with financial vision.

Discover Your Destiny During College

Everything just started happening! I realized that Jesus had an energy for the project and I was just trying to keep up with what He was already doing there!

—Sarah Aulie, "Handmade Hope"
Radiant Magazine, Winter 2007
(Orlando, FL: Relevant Media Group), Fall 2007.

I RECENTLY TALKED WITH ABBEY Hazelbaker, a student who was finishing up prerequisite courses for an orthotics and prosthetics program. I asked about her career decision, why she had decided to go in this direction. She began describing her experience with having treatment for scoliosis, for her a severe curvature of the spine. During that experience, she had spent a great deal of time in the medical atmosphere. While she was watching and listening in that environment, God was growing within her a passion to help people with similar pain and experiences.

She closed our conversation with, "Now I see that it had to do with my calling." She didn't see her experiences as random or negative, even though she could have viewed them as such. She could tell that God's hand was guiding her, even during the hard times. She could say with confidence, "God meant my experience for good." For Abbey, the hard decision of transferring to a new school, leaving her comfort zones of friends and situations, and entering something completely new was "all to pursue God's calling in my life."* With

---

* *Quotes used with the permission of Abbey Hazelbaker.*

passion and focus like that, Abbey's destined to fulfill her unique mission in life!

When you choose to live life inspired and to ask God for your destiny, you will find that He has an energy for certain tasks. He will place you in certain circumstances to develop new desires and qualities within your heart. He will help you get new abilities. He has a mission he'd like to use you to accomplish, so why wouldn't He equip you? When you ask Him, he'll begin to show you the mission that he's placed within you.

Today's Destiny

Living your destiny during college begins by understanding the opportunity for personal growth before you this very moment and seeing God's plan at work in your life today. Destiny is not just reaching your goal or the fulfillment of a desire; it's trusting God during the process of growth. It's the stretching of your heart, the testing of your faith. It's living with integrity in the details of your life regardless of the consequences or situation, because destiny, God's best for your life, and integrity are inseparable.

To get an idea of the potential you have during college to discover your mission, what God would like you to do, take a look through the lens of Arthur Chickering's research on college student development. He found that students grow in seven primary areas during college:

- Developing Competence
- Managing Emotions
- Moving through Autonomy toward Interdependence
- Developing Mature Interpersonal Relationships
- Establishing Identity
- Developing Purpose
- Developing Integrity[1]

Just by reading his categories you can see the parts of your life that are influenced during college. So as you continue with your undergraduate years, take careful note of how you are changing in each area of your life.

Develop Your Ability

Professors often describe learning as a measurable change in behavior. What they're saying is that when you complete a class, your thinking and your behavior should be different. When you graduate, you should be a more developed "you" than when you came in. We should see a recognizable growth in how you communicate, problem-solve, relate to others, and act. Because, as you learn, your actions change to reflect your new thoughts.

Your courses, including your general education courses, are providing you with the opportunity to learn skills to complement your strengths. Even as you learn the specialized language in your major courses, your perception of, and your approach to, the world around you will begin to change. You might begin to see life through the eyes of a psychologist—understanding behavior, relationships, and mental processes. Or maybe you'll see like an architect—envisioning buildings and needed internal structural changes.

As your thoughts about yourself, your environment, and others are heightened, your actions change to reflect these new thoughts. If your perspective about music is enhanced, the desire to more fully master your instrument will follow. Your skills will change to match the desire that you have to share your art with others. As you continue your studies with computer science, you'll take your programming skills to the next level so you can bring a new approach to the field. If you've been called to be a physical therapist, then your training will make your job a reality.

Developing your skills is important for your success both during and after college. Asher in *How to Get Any Job with Any Major* describes the qualities employers are looking for when hiring. The list reads: communication skills, honesty/integrity, teamwork skills, interpersonal skills, motivation/initiative, strong work ethic, analytical skills, flexibility/adaptability, computer skills, and self-confidence.[2] These are qualities that we can all strengthen and use in any setting. Don't don't wait for your professors to motivate you to develop these skills; motivate yourself to learn and to gain the knowledge you need for success. Proverbs 19:2 says, "It is not good to have zeal without knowledge..." Directionless passion is a waste of good energy so do what it takes to develop a strong skill set.

I had a professor who believed strongly that competence, developing your ability, creates confidence. If you want to increase your confidence, gain new ways of problem solving, he would say. Master your subject area, and you'll feel more confident. Practice your communication skills, and you'll use them more. When you do your best by sharpening your ability, your confidence will grow, and more importantly, you will start to see your dreams become reality.

Successful students do what it takes to live out their potential without letting their confidence mutate into arrogance. Do your best to see the potential for personal growth in each course that you take, and look for ways to improve your physical state by developing good habits so that you will have the energy to do your best. As a Christian, let your motivation develop your potential; without comparing yourself to others, illustrate that your faith is alive. Most importantly, remember that your willingness to be used by God is far more important than your own ability or skills. Being available for use is always more essential than competence.

Spirit-led Emotions

We've all wasted time by mistaking our emotions for our spirituality. We often act on our own feelings, confusing them with steps of faith. Put that behind you during college. Living inspired goes beyond natural impulse or dark emotions; it means living a life listening to God's voice.

I have a friend who is a counselor, and he describes emotions as neutral; they simply give us the capacity to feel. It's our thoughts that are positive or negative. If you'd like to experience a positive sense of well-being, then choose positive thoughts. If you obsess about the future and let anxiety get the best of you, then live the verse: "Do not be anxious about anything, but in everything, by prayer and petition, with thanksgiving, present your requests to

God. And the peace of God, which transcends all understanding, will guard your hearts and your minds in Christ Jesus" (Philippians 4:6-7). To deal with anxiety I often think about eternity. There is no pace within eternity, only life. When I imagine eternity and pour my heart out to God, my mind is sustained in peace. If you're stuck in the past and feel like you can't move beyond something, then live here: "But one thing I do: Forgetting what is behind and straining toward what is ahead, I press on toward the goal to win the prize for which God has called me heavenward in Christ Jesus. All of us who are mature should take such a view of things" (Philippians 3:13-15).

Our emotions are fueled by our thoughts, so we must choose the right thoughts in each situation so that our emotions will keep in step with reality. During conflict with your roommate, if you'll let your thoughts be motivated by God, your emotions and words will experience spiritual guidance instead of cloudy, impulsive emotions and words. To think spiritually and to master the emotions that keep us down, our beliefs must be based upon the stability of His transcendental perspective. If we'll let "love, joy, peace, patience, kindness, goodness, faithfulness, gentleness, and self-control" fuel our emotions, we can step back and watch as our old, confusing emotions lose their power (Galatians 5:22-23). To overcome anxiety, beat depression, and to balance your highs and lows, choose to take the spiritual approach. The power that God supplies is sufficient to help you choose right things and to avoid being duped by your emotions: "But you will receive power when the Holy Spirit comes on you" (Acts 1:8).

During college, get to know your personality and how you respond to people and situations. Ask God to give you a fresh perspective of biblical spirituality, not emotionalism. I asked a dentist once about the stress of the exams he took in preparation for dental school. He said, "All I could do was my best. I know what Revelation says. I know that God is coming back for us, and what will matter most is that I did my best for Him." His ability to think realistically, by placing his entire life in spiritual context, calmed his nerves and helped him stay focused on his priorities. He did his personal best without obsessing or fixating on knowledge that he might not have. He stayed realistic.

Learning to recognize and understand emotion in ourselves and in others is important for our spiritual lives. We've been blessed with the capacity to experience joy, compassion, peace, gratitude, and love. When these noble themes stir within us, we're motivated to live with determined, balanced vision. Do your homework with your emotions. Get help with how you experience life. For starters, read *Happiness is a Choice* by Drs. Minirth and Meier[3] or Dr. Colbert's *Deadly Emotions.*[4] (See page *try* Stress Management for more tips.)

Independence and Community

When you're maturing, you're growing in your desire for community. It's critical to take responsibility for yourself, but living in community means that you see the significance of living connected for the sake of a common good.

Living with interdependence means you're using your spiritual talent for the benefit of others. You're allowing the Spirit to work through you to bring out their best, and your potential is encouraged because of their gifts.

Adrian Rogers, in *What Every Christian Ought to Know*, breaks commonwealth gifts into three basic types:

- Teaching/Leadership
- Service Gifts
- Sign Gifts[5]

To live out the body of Christ, we need these spiritual gifts working together because we know that "there are different kinds of gifts but the same Spirit. There are different kinds of service but the same Lord. There are different kinds of working, but the same God works all of them in all men." (1 Corinthians 12: 4-7). If you have been given a higher nature in Jesus, the continual cause of your spiritual life, then He has given you a supernatural talent, a gift that has life-giving ability. When you're spiritually active during college, you allow His Spirit to work through you to help others. There's safety in a multitude of counselors because you're engaging the body of Christ, not just the insight of one.

Living connected means you have freedom from people-pleasing and that you can live listening to His voice. It means you value the use of spiritual gifts, and you see the urgent need for Christian students to use these gifts. If Christian students would simply meet with a willingness and intent to serve, lead, teach, give, encourage, and discern, we could watch as darkness lifts from the hearts and minds of the students, staff, professors, and communities of your campus.

I heard someone on the radio once say that our lives are like cups with holes in them. When we're filled, we leak. To continually live at our best, we need God's continual flow of grace. We need to stay next to our Source so we can remain filled with His good. We have a need for God, and He enjoys having a relationship with us. So as you continue to live filled with His presence, endeavor to let others experience His healing touch through you during college.

Develop Mature Relationship

If you're growing in wisdom and understanding, then you're growing socially. Solomon received "largeness of heart like the sand on the seashore" when he asked God for wisdom (1 Kings 4:29, NKJV). If wisdom is our aim during college, then, like Solomon, our hearts should be growing larger for others.

Our heart for God is always reflected in our willingness to love others, to regard them above ourselves. We should always keep before us the awareness that our relationships are never random; they are designed. Our need and desire for relationship reveals to us the heart of our Maker. The symmetry of His design for His creation includes harmony in relationships. That's why a greater understanding of relationship always follows wisdom. A heart for others, to think less about ourselves, is how the world sees clearly who we are and the Creator of relationship.

Healthy relationships challenge us, bring us healing and strength, help us to grow, and they allow us to experience God in a new way. Mature relationships are creative, enjoyable, deep, forgiving, marked by truth, loving, selfless, and lived out in reality. These relationships are always the result of mature individuals. So don't be surprised when you gain freedom from always needing the approval of others as you grow in your understanding of mature relationships, because you're learning to value others and their ideas without relying primarily on them for strength or happiness.

Alexander Astin, in *What Matters in College,* says that your "...peer group is the single most potent source of influence on growth and development in the undergraduate years."[6] Our peers can make or break us in the personal best department. Mature people promote well-being in our lives, and college is the perfect time to realize this and work at creating beneficial relationships. To make the most of college, learn to develop mature relationships with the right kinds of people. To get you started on developing these kinds of relationships, try reading Drs. Cloud and Townsend's books on *Boundaries*[7] or Les and Leslie Parrott's book *Relationships*[8], and see page 130 for a few conflict management tips.

Live Your Identity

Living your identity is the most important issue you face as a college student. To know who you are, you must first answer the call to a relationship with God. It is only through this relationship that you can discover your true identity and what you've been uniquely called to do.

An accurate self-concept begins by knowing God, and a clear picture of you is maintained by listening to and obeying Him. When you know that He loves you and that He is passionate about your future, you'll be motivated to live up to His expectations. If you see yourself the way He does, then you will have an excellent understanding of your purpose, and your spiritual destiny. As you live your identity in God, you'll be at peace with your lifestyle because you'll be integrated and whole. You'll be the person that you were meant to be.

Students who live their identity, instead of socially scripted lives, have excellent views on sexuality. They know,

There's more to sex than skin on skin. Sex is as much spiritual mystery as physical fact. As written in Scripture, 'The two become one.' Since we want to become spiritually one with the Master, we must not pursue the kind of sex that avoids commitment and intimacy, leaving us more lonely than ever—the kind of sex that can never 'become one'" (1 Cor. 6:15-17 The Message).

These same students, who know that sex is about marriage and marriage is about cultivating our relationship with God, recognize that the decisions they make reflect their identity and that their daily purpose is to live their new, spiritual identity (Galatians 2:20).

Your identity as a child of God will be threatened at every turn during college. Know who you are. Do what it takes to protect the condition of your heart so that you can see clearly the life you have been called to. As you're living like this, your growth will be based on truth, and you'll be able to reach your full potential.

Your identity, rather who God is to you, is the central concern of your life. It is in relationship with the same Mind who created the universe that you will begin to understand that He has a unique mission for you, one that involves helping meet the deepest needs of others in a setting that He places you in. Living your identity, which involves listening daily to His voice, will ensure that you live your purpose.

Live Your Purpose

Discovering your destiny during college is less about finding your ideal job someday and more about being your ideal person. We often obsess about building fantastic careers with little consideration of who we are or what God would like for us to do.

Arthur Miller, Jr., says, "We cannot become anything we want. In truth, we cannot become anything other than who we already are, if we wish to be fulfilled in our lives and vocation. We must stop trying to 'become' something else, or to 'develop' or 'cultivate' some trait that we fundamentally lack, and instead start *being* who we already are by identifying our giftedness and living it out."[9] He's not saying that we can't sharpen our skills, but he is saying that we can't fundamentally change our personal design. We have to be who we have been designed to be, people of destiny with individual missions.

God has built purpose into each of us. He has gifted us with a unique mission and the spiritual ability to carry out His plan. College is simply an opportunity to ask Him to help you see the gift that He has placed within you and to lead you into the place where He wants to use that gift. Richard Bolles says your unique mission in life is:

1. to exercise that Talent which you particularly came to Earth to use.
2. in those place(s) or setting(s) which God has caused to appeal to you the most,
3. and for those purposes which God most needs to have done in the world.[10]

The most fulfilling place to be in life is living God's design for you, the place where your relationship with Him inspires you to use your gifts to accomplish His purpose. You have a unique mission within you, a mission that communicates His purpose to the world. Oswald Chambers adds, "As long as you maintain your own personal interests and ambitions, you cannot be completely aligned or identified with God's interests. This can only be accomplished by giving up all of your personal plans once and for all, and by allowing God to take you directly into His purpose for the world."[11]

To live out your destiny, your unique ministry to the world, you must look to God as your guide. When you humble yourself before Him in all that you do, you will not be easily distracted from this purpose. You'll be able to focus on what you're here to accomplish, like ServiceMaster, a Fortune 500 company. Take a look at their objectives:

- "To honor God in all we do"
- "To help people develop"
- "To pursue excellence"
- "To grow profitably"[12]

People of destiny are not easily diverted when it comes to accomplishing their objectives. They know who they are, what their talent is, how to wait on God, how to strive, and how to be content with where God places them. They honor God in everything they do. He adds success to their company or endeavor. God placed the gift of art within my dad, gave him the spiritual gift of teaching, and then guided him into the place where He most needed him. Dad didn't want to change his mission. God entrusted him with art for the purpose of helping others in the same way that ServiceMaster has been given the ability to create and maintain a large organization.

We've been designed with a unique purpose. It's our responsibility to discover it. Solomon tells us that, "It is the glory of God to conceal a matter; to search out a matter is the glory of kings" (Proverb 25:2). We should ask ourselves these questions as we pursue that purpose: What purpose has been placed within my heart? With what gifts have I been entrusted? In what setting does He want me use these gifts? What mission does He want to accomplish?

Live Integrity

In the end, your skills will not hold your destiny together. Your social connections will not. Your family will not. Your money will not. But your integrity will. Integrity is simply living consistent with your God-given identity. It's being true to your new self.

When given the opportunity to ask for anything, listen to Solomon's request and God's reply:

> *Solomon*: "So give your servant a discerning heart to govern your people and to distinguish between right and wrong. For who is able to govern this great people of yours?"
>
> *God*: "Since you have asked for this and not for long life or wealth for yourself, nor have asked for the death of your enemies but for discernment in administering justice, I will do what you have asked. I will give you a wise and discerning heart, so that there will never have been anyone like you, nor will there ever be. Moreover, I will give you what you have not asked for—both riches and honor—so that in your lifetime you will have no equal among kings. And if you walk in my ways and obey my statutes and commands as David your father did, I will give you a long life" (1 Kings 3:9-14).

Solomon knew that only a life of integrity, making sound moral decisions, would cause him to live out his mission as king. He knew leading a kingdom was best done with integrity. Herbert Spencer, the English philosopher, says, "Not education but character is man's greatest need and man's greatest safeguard."[13] As leaders, our greatest need is character. Our purpose is to live daily with integrity. If we live with integrity God Himself will be our safeguard.

All areas of your growth as a student hinge on your integrity. That's why Proverbs 4:23 says, "Above all else, guard your heart, for it is the wellspring of life." When we keep a clear conscience, we stay connected to truth which helps us make the choices that cause us to discover our full potential. If we'll live with protected hearts, then we'll know how to best develop the talents and relationships we've been given.

Your priority as a student is to live consistent with your identity in the seemingly small areas during college: with your finances, talents, decisions, sexuality, and relationships. What you accomplish in college and in your life will simply reflect the character of your heart.

Anyone can build a career, but few live a destiny. Your true success during and after college is a matter of your heart. IQ is important. EQ is significant, but ultimately it's your integrity that matters most.

How not to discover your destiny...

"I've learned one thing, and that's to quit worrying about stupid things. You have four years to be irresponsible here. Relax. Work is for people with jobs. You'll never remember class time, but you'll remember time you wasted hanging out with your friends. So, stay out late. Go out on a Tuesday with your friends when you have a paper due Wednesday. Spend money you don't have. Drink 'til sunrise. The work never ends, but college does..."

—Tom Petty[14]

If this is your mentality during college, then don't be surprised when you find yourself at graduation with little understanding of what God's purpose is for your life. If you are planting seeds of irre-sponsibility and drunkenness, then why would you hope to reap responsible and trustworthy behavior, much less clear direction? College *is* the real world, and I'm tired of people making it out to be less real than other social environments. Just because you're not making as much money as you might be someday, doesn't make your experience any less real. You're in the real world with real consequences, so don't let anyone tell you otherwise. It's time to step up and develop realistic, principled thinking.

It's good to be young and to experience new things during college. We know that we can "be happy, young man, while you are young, and let your heart give you joy in the days of your youth. Follow the ways of your heart and whatever your eyes see…" We have been given permission to have a great time and to live with a sense of wonder. But we should also remember the second part of that verse: "…know that for all these things God will bring you to judg-ment" (Ecclesiastes 11:9). Just because you're young and enjoying college doesn't mean that everything you do will be beneficial to you or to others. Consider your future; don't miss your destiny: "…ask where the good way is, and walk in it" (Psalm 6:16). Oswald Chambers puts it best: "If I obey Jesus Christ, the redemption of God will flow through me to the lives of others, because behind the deed of obedience is the reality of Almighty God. As soon as I obey Him, I fulfill my spiritual destiny."[15]

Fulfill your spiritual destiny by being obedient to God during college. Listen to Him, and you'll go beyond what you've imagined for your future. You are not the same person that you were in high school; you're growing. Give yourself the freedom to change for the better at any time. Don't let your past be your future by continuing to see your world through your childhood eyes. Live inspired. When you do, your influence will be eternal because you'll live with higher purpose. Your integrity will be sound because you'll view college as a chapter in your spiritual journey. Your destiny will be realized because you obey God.

try Destiny Living

1. Will you let God use you at full capacity by living your identity during college?
2. Get busy with searching out your talent and where best to use what you've been given. Calling is drawing close to God and listening to Him on where to be and how to be while you're there.
3. Read page 114-115 for tips on how to prepare spiritually for college and life transitions.
4. Pray for a friend. Let her know that you are praying that she will develop her talent and know which direction to take as she uses her gifts.
5. Be a trendsetter in your family. Don't go to college just thinking about yourself or the money you're going to make someday. Go with purpose. Go with a vision for your life, your family, and for the lives of others. Go knowing that God has a unique purpose for your being here.

try Inspired

"We are not *try*ing to please men, but God who tests the heart."
—(1 Thessalonians 2:4; emphasis added)

L IVING INSPIRED DURING COLLEGE is not the easy thing to do. If it were, every student would be living higher and doing his best to please God. Being inspired involves saying no to empty social scripts, ideas, and behaviors. Being inspired involves saying yes to living out your true story. Inspiration—destiny living—is living for God with all that you are.

God is your guide during college. He is here, this very moment, guiding you. If you have given your heart to Him, then He is within you, motivating and leading you. He has a higher purpose for you during college, so don't waste your time and good energy in darkness. He has given you the opportunity to shine and to do small things with big heart. Let Him find you faithful with the hidden details of your life. Let Him increase your influence so you can bring His light to others. Step out in truth in your courses and on campus by letting others experience Jesus through your love and insight.

Students who try higher share three common characteristics.

1. They live their identity.
   - They receive identity and purpose through relationship with the Creator.
   - They know who they are, so they live with daily purpose.
   - They live with integrity and excellence in the details.
   - They listen to their Guide.

2. Choose a spiritual perspective.
    •   They see college as a calling.
    •   They see the depth of their experiences.
    •   They see how people and circumstances are connected.
    •   They see reality, so they're practical.

3. They live inspired.
    •   They encourage others to pursue their dreams and passion.
    •   They take small, consistent steps toward their vision.
    •   They are motivated by the Spirit and guided by His principles.
    •   They make the most of their opportunities.

Listen to what these students, true spiritual leaders, had to say when asked about trying college God's way:

> "Trying college God's way means to basically go into your college experience with an open mind and an open heart for what He may have in store. You have to be flexible to God's will because He could change your plans with the weather. If you allow yourself to get stubborn or question everything that is happening, you may end up missing out on a blessing."
>
> —Torrey

> "Well, in my opinion, when you 'try college God's way' I think that as you go through college, you live a life for Christ. For me, being raised as a Christian, and knowing that we are called to live as Christ would and to be a light for him in a dark world (be in this world, but not of the world) doing the drinking and partying just seems to contradict. Now, it doesn't stop there. Because you have the opportunity to go to college, not everyone does, putting your full effort into it seems like it is something God would expect from someone doing it His way."
>
> —Kyle

God will tell you what steps to take concerning your course work, your major, and your future. He will guide you to the right friends, so be willing to listen. He will provide for you along the way, so be willing to ask for the right things and with the right motive. He knows your heart, and He wants to guide you on the path that He has chosen for you. As you transition through college, don't force decisions. Rely on His wisdom because "…without faith it is impossible to please Him, for he who comes to God must believe that He is and that He is a rewarder of those who seek Him" (Hebrews 11:6, NASB). Listen to Him about your calling, and you'll experience His best for you:

> "It seems like every time one door closes in my face another one opens right back up. When I feel like I'm at my wit's end, God just seems to turn it right around. It seems like God has guided me to different means of serving him as well as others while on campus. I'm an active member in Inspirational Singers, our university's gospel choir, and I can't say enough about how much this experience has been a blessing to me and my college career socially, spiritually and even financially! It has allowed me to meet other students that share the same love for Christ that I do and understand the struggles that sometimes arise for Christians on a college campus. It provided me with a scholarship to help out with my college expenses and it also provided me with an opportunity to take my first trip outside of the country. I never thought that I would travel to Beijing, China during my freshman year of college but…that just goes to show how much of a blessed time you can have in college if you just let God use you.
>
> –Torrey*

God has guided me not only during college, but throughout my entire life. During school He has guided me financially, socially, and personally. He has guided me first off, by allowing me to know my major of choice since I was very young. Putting me in that department allowed me to receive great financial help with funding school. Socially, God has placed several different organizations on campus that allowed me to meet great Christian people who have helped me keep my life focused and centered on Christ. On a personal standpoint, He has given me the strength to follow Him and not fall in to wicked things that are always present while at school…has allowed me to keep my personal relationship with Him strong.

—Kyle*

---

*Quotes used with the permission of Torrey Eason and Kyle Kleber.

When you choose to live with integrity and excellence during college, God will use it for good. I've known people who were in college for one semester before God called them to a different task. He is using that one semester in ways they never imagined. Maybe you'll complete a two-year program, a four-year degree, or a graduate or professional degree. If you are called to a program, God will sustain you and help you see it through to completion. There is no anxiety involved, only trust, knowing that He will give you the strength and ability to make good choices to succeed. If you want to more fully understand your destiny after graduation, then practice your purpose now. Ask for His wisdom, and He will take care of where you carry out your mission. Make the most of every semester, every opportunity, and remember that being our best for God is living our destiny. So why not, like these students, risk letting God be your guide during college?

Your Future

So there is hope for your future (Jeremiah 31:17).

...she did not consider her future. Her fall was astounding (Lamentations 1:9).

try Wisdom

I have more insight than all my teachers, for I meditate on your statutes (Psalm 119:99).

Surely you desire truth in the inner parts, you teach me wisdom in the inmost place (Psalm 51:6).

try Reality

See to it that no one takes you captive through hollow and deceptive philosophy, which depends on human tradition and the basic principles of this world rather than on Christ (Colossians 2:8).

When the Counselor comes, whom I will send to you from the Father, the Spirit of truth who goes out from the Father... (John 15:26).

So then, brothers, stand firm and hold to the teaching we passed on to you... (2 Thessalonians 2:15).

try Learning

Let the wise listen and add to their learning, and let the discerning get guidance (Proverbs 1:5).

It is the glory of God to conceal a matter; to search out a matter is the glory of kings (Proverbs 25:2).

Apply your heart to instruction and your ears to words of knowledge (Proverbs 23:12).

The heart of the discerning acquires knowledge; the ears of the wise seek it out (Proverbs 18:15).

A fool finds no pleasure in understanding but delights in airing his own opinions (Proverbs 18:2).

Since my youth, O God, you have taught me (Psalm 71:17).

try Spiritual Decisions

You, my brothers, were called to be free. But do not use your freedom to indulge the sinful nature; rather, serve one another in love (Galatians 5:13).

It is for freedom that Christ has set us free. Stand firm, then, and do not let yourselves be burdened again by a yoke of slavery (Galatians 5:1).

...for the Lord searches every heart and understands every motive behind the thoughts (1 Chronicles 28:9).

...ask where the good way is, and walk in it (Jeremiah 6:16).

You are my help and my deliverer (Psalm 70:5).

try Trust: Decision, Major, and Career

The Lord will guide you always... (Isaiah 58:11).

Show me the way I should go, for to you I lift up my soul (Psalm 143:8b).

He will instruct him in the way chosen for him (Psalm 25:12).

Direct my footsteps according to your word (Psalm 119:133).

I know, O Lord, that a man's life is not his own; it is not for man to direct his steps (Jeremiah 10:23).

I will praise the Lord, who counsels me; even at night my heart instructs me (Psalm 16:7).

I will instruct you and teach you in the way you should go; I will counsel you and watch over you (Psalm 32:8).

Make plans by seeking advice; if you wage war, obtain guidance (Proverbs 20:18).

He guides the humble in what is right and teaches them his way (Psalm 25:9).

Since you are my rock and my fortress, for the sake of your name lead and guide me (Psalm 31:3).

try Building Your Skills

For this reason I remind you to fan into flame the gift of God, which is in you through the laying on of my hands (2 Timothy 1:6).

Not that we are competent in ourselves to claim anything for ourselves, but our competence comes from God (2 Corinthians 3:5).

try Spiritual Influence

He who loves a pure heart and whose speech is gracious will have the king for his friend (Proverbs 22:11).

...power belongs to God (Psalm 62:11, ESV).

You will increase my honor (Psalm 71:21).

...I declare your power to the next generation, your might to all who are to come (Psalm 71:18).

Don't let anyone look down on you because you are young, but set an example for the believers in speech, in life, in love, in faith and in purity (1 Timothy 4:12).

try Communicating

The tongue has the power of life and death, and those who love it will eat its fruit (Proverbs 18:21).

My heart is stirred by a noble theme as I recite verses for the king; my tongue is the pen of a skillful writer (Psalm 45:1).

The mouth of the righteous man utters wisdom, and his tongue speaks what is just (Psalm 37:30).

Let your conversation be always full of grace, seasoned with salt, so that you may know how to answer everyone (Colossians 4:6).

try Listening

Blessed is the man who listens to me, watching daily at my doors, waiting at my doorway (Proverbs 8:34).

The way of a fool seems right to him, but a wise man listens to advice (Proverbs 12:15).

Stop listening to instruction, my son, and you will stray from the words of knowledge. (Proverbs 19:27).

try Spiritual Success

Humility and the fear of the Lord bring wealth and honor and life (Proverbs 22:4).

A generous man will himself be blessed, for he shares his food with the poor (Proverbs 22:9).

Do not wear yourself out to get rich; have the wisdom to show restraint (Proverbs 23:4).

Do not join those who drink too much wine or gorge themselves on meat, for drunkards and gluttons become poor, and drowsiness clothes them in rags (Proverbs 23:20-21).

...your God has set you above your companions by anointing you with the oil of joy (Psalm 45:7).

May the favor of the Lord our God rest upon us; establish the work of our hands for us—yes, establish the work of our hands (Psalm 90:17).

...but those who hope in the Lord will renew their strength. They will soar on wings like eagles; they will run and not grow weary, they will walk and not be faint (Isaiah 40:31).

I am the Lord, the God of all mankind. Is anything too hard for me? (Jeremiah 32:27).

try Relationship

If one falls down, his friend can help him up. But pity the man who falls and has no one to help him up! (Ecclesiastes 4:10).

He who covers over an offense promotes love, but whoever repeats the matter separates close friends (Proverbs 17:9).

"Honor your father and mother"—which is the first commandment with a promise—"that it may go well with you and that you may enjoy long life on the earth" (Ephesians 6: 1-3).

Charm is deceptive, and beauty is fleeting; but a woman who fears the Lord is to be praised (Proverbs 31:30).

…for the Father himself loves you, because you have loved me and have believed that I came from God (John 16:27, ESV).

try Personal Management

Go to the ant, you sluggard; consider its ways and be wise! It has no commander, no overseer or ruler, yet it stores its provisions in summer and gathers its food at harvest (Proverbs 6:6-8).

Teach us to number our days aright, that we may gain a heart of wisdom (Psalm 90:12).

try Your Identity Instead of Alcohol

Wine is a mocker and beer a brawler; whoever is led astray by them is not wise (Proverbs 20:1).

Woe to those who rise early in the morning to run after their drinks, who stay up late at night till they are inflamed with wine (Isaiah 5:11).

Woe to those who are heroes at drinking wine and champions at mixing drinks (Isaiah 5:22).

Who has woe? Who has sorrow? Who has strife? Who has complaints? Who has needless bruises? Who has bloodshot eyes? Those who linger over wine, who go to sample bowls of mixed wine. Do not gaze at wine when it is red, when it sparkles in the cup, when it goes down smoothly! In the end it bites like a snake and poisons like a viper. Your eyes will see strange sights and your mind imagine confusing things. You will be like one sleeping on the high seas, lying on top of the rigging. 'They hit me,' you will say, 'but I'm not hurt! They beat me, but I don't feel it! When will I wake up so I can find another drink?' (Proverbs 23:29-35).

try Your True Sexuality

...but I will not be mastered by anything. "Food for the stomach and the stomach for food"—but God will destroy them both. The body is not meant for sexual immorality, but for the Lord, and the Lord for the body (1 Corinthians 6:12-13).

try Destiny Living

For this reason, make every effort to add to your faith goodness; and to goodness, knowledge, and to knowledge, self control; and to self-control, perseverance; and to perseverance, godliness; and to godliness, brotherly kindness; and to brotherly kindness, love. For if you possess these qualities in increasing measure, they will keep you from being ineffective and unproductive in your knowledge of our Lord Jesus Christ. But if anyone does not have them, he is nearsighted and blind, and has forgotten that he has been cleansed from his past sins. Therefore, my brothers, be all the more eager to make your calling and election sure. For if you do these things, you will never fall, and you will receive a rich welcome into the eternal kingdom of our Lord and Savior Jesus Christ (2 Peter 1:3).

try Prayer

God, guide me during college. My life is not my own. I know you have a purpose for me. Help me to know which path to take and to see the opportunity I have to please you. Guide me in the way that you have chosen for me.

try Exploring Your Major

YOUR MAJOR IS IMPORTANT to God. He wants you to study information that inspires you to do your best and to shape the mind He has given you. Talk with advisors from the departments that interest you. Get a feel for the opportunities within the department and ask them about what some of their graduates are doing now. Research online what types of jobs are available for a degree in that field. Can you see yourself in that type of work? Will your talents and motivation for that subject meet the demands of the coursework involved in completing that major?

To begin exploring your major, an area of study that will challenge you to live your full potential, try using your catalog of studies. Flip through it, taking note of the various colleges or departments. Decide which departments are most interesting to you. Then, find a list of all of the majors and minors your school offers. Go through the list, circling all of the majors that seem interesting. Look for patterns in your decisions. Which are most appealing and for what reasons? Have you primarily circled science or math related majors? Or humanities, philosophy, and English-based courses? Business oriented? Health? Architecture? Engineering? Education? Agricultural? Or social science majors? Once you have somewhat narrowed your list, flip to the course descriptions, and read about the types of courses you would take in these majors. Does the information have a pull to it? Can you see yourself devoting a semester to one of the courses? A year to the courses?

Remember that all majors have something in common: they give you training in how to be a learner for life. You develop a core set of skills. They teach you how to break tasks into workable parts, how to organize and retain information, and how to analyze problems and create solutions. You also develop communication skills while writing papers, learning a specialized language, giving presentations, and working in groups. As you explore your major, keep in mind that you can use the skills that you learn in any major to pursue your unique mission.

Appendix 2

try College with Purpose

GETTING A HIGHER EDUCATION is important on many levels. College can help you enlarge your vision for your future, provide you with knowledge and the opportunity to develop your ability, help you write and speak with clarity, understand complex theories and concepts, and enhance your perspective of others, your community, and the world. As you continue with college, clarify your purpose and motivation by answering these questions:

1. What's the purpose of college? For me? For society?
2. Why did I decide to attend college? What's my motivation for being here?
3. Have I been listening to God about my daily purpose? What has He said to you today?
4. Have I talked with someone about God's plan for my life?
5. What do I hope to accomplish my first semester? During my four years here? After college?
6. What steps will I take to ensure that I succeed in college?

try A College Plan

WRITING OUT A PLAN for your life is one of the best ways to clarify your priorities and challenge yourself to live to the fullest. In his book *Life on the Edge,* Dr. James Dobson refers to the ages between 16 and 26 as the "critical decade" because so many major life decisions are made during this time.[1] This is the best time for you to learn how to develop a plan and see it through by sticking with your principles. If you will choose to make excellent choices during these critical years, you will have the makings of a sound foundation from which to build your 20s and 30s.

When building an academic plan, make sure to talk with your academic counselor about creating an outline for your four years in college. Write out when you will take general education classes, major requirements, and electives (courses toward your minor or pre-professional courses). What courses can you take that will help you develop your strengths, your unique gifts? Talk with mentors and counselors about how to develop your leadership ability. Get around experts in the areas in which you are interested. Build your leadership skills. Work them often. Do not expect to improve if you never put your skills into action. Learn to improve from each experience.

Academic Plan

	1st Year	2nd Year	3rd Year	4th Year
Courses 1st Semester	1. 2. 3. 4. 5. 6.	1. 2. 3. 4. 5. 6.	1. 2. 3. 4. 5. 6.	1. 2. 3. 4. 5. 6.
Courses 2nd Semester	1. 2. 3. 4. 5. 6.	1. 2. 3. 4. 5. 6.	1. 2. 3. 4. 5. 6.	1. 2. 3. 4. 5. 6.
My Summer plans:				
My Critique: • Is my plan balanced? • Are my courses challenging, but manageable? • Am I motivated by my choices? • Do my courses develop my talent? • Have I discussed my plan with advisor?				

Leadership Plan

1. Research your opportunities for servant-leadership by talking with your academic and career advisors.
2. Be creative when developing your plan. For instance, did you know that Prison Fellowship Ministries has internship opportunities?
3. Be balanced. One leadership position can outweigh a large number of volunteer experiences.
4. Update your experiences on your resume. Keep notes on what you learn in a journal.

	1st Year	2nd Year	3rd Year	4th Year
Volunteer Experience				
Internship Experience				
Work Experience				
Career Shadowing				
Honors				
Training				
Other				

Plan Weekly

1. Develop a tentative weekly plan by blocking out time.
2. Block out your priorities first.
3. Break assignments into workable parts throughout the week.

Monday	Tuesday	Wednesday	Thursday	Friday	Saturday	Sunday
7:00 am						
8:00						
9:00						
10:00						
11:00						
12:00 pm						
1:00						
2:00						
3:00						
4:00						
5:00						
6:00						
7:00						
8:00						
9:00						
10:00						
Priorities						
To Do List						

try Focused Motivation!

Step 1: State the assignment that you'd like to get done. Examples:
    a) Write an 8-10 page paper using APA on "Rites of Passage" for your anthropology class.
    b) Create a PowerPoint presentation on mission statements for your management course.
    c) Draw a sample of blood from a patient and write your report according to the ABO system indicating presence or absence of Rh factor.

Step 2: Make a list of the knowledge and skills you need to accomplish the assignment. Break the assignment into workable parts.

Step 3: Create a timeline for the assignment and get started on it.

Step 4: Evaluate your process and improve it for the next time.

   *See Focused Motivation: Paper Example. (Adapted from James O. Hammons Steps in Performing a Task Analysis)[1]

Focused Motivation: Paper Example

My Task (be exact): I'm going to write a 10-page research paper on Emotional Intelligence using APA guidelines in three weeks.

My Needs (list):
- Need to know my purpose/goals for writing the paper

- Need to know how to use APA format
- Need to know more about Emotional Intelligence
- Need to know how to write a good paragraph/research paper
- Need to turn in on time
- Need to do my best and trust God to guide me with my thoughts

My Plan:

- Ask God to help me do my best and to stay motivated
- Write truth; keep in mind my values and worldview
- Talk with writing center; get a one-page summary on using APA
- Get a handout on writing good paragraphs and research papers
- Talk with reference librarian on researching topic
- Research topic
- Create timeline
  Week 1: Create plan, gather resources, and outline paper.
  Week 2: Write rough draft.
  Week 3: Review paper. Have someone else read it. Turn in.

Evaluate My Process (when finished):

- What would I do differently?
- How efficient was I?
- Did I do my best with the time I was given?
- Did I accomplish my purpose for writing the paper?

Evaluate!

Create

Make

State

try 5 Reasons— College Students Succeed

DURING A DISCUSSION WITH several other advisors about why students succeed, we tossed around five areas that influence success in college. The list is not comprehensive, but it does give some insight into what many of us have seen in students who succeed. I've given the areas my own take.

1. Know Purpose...

They know why they're in college. They see college as a calling. They know they're here to grow in their faith. They know the importance of gaining new skills or enhancing old ones. They know the benefits of being here.

2. Life Management...

They have a Godly perspective of time, and they develop the skills to make sure that they live out their purpose. They make the most of their time. They learn ways to keep organized. They have specific strategies for listening to lectures, taking notes, reading assignments, and writing papers.

3. Best Major...

They ask God to guide them into the major that's best for them. They act and plan with wisdom. They do their research, talk with their academic and career counselors, complete personality inventories, and career assessments. They find a major that they enjoy and that complements their ability. They're taking courses in which they can succeed. They're not forcing a major (*e.g.*, they don't dread every semester, they find the courses they're taking engaging, and they have the ability to do well in their major courses; their major energizes them).

4. Are Involved...

They see getting involved as essential to their purpose in college. They know it will positively influence their campus and community. They talk with professors, other students, and staff at their school. They don't wait to feel connected; they take initiative to connect with the campus. They check-in with their academic counselors and other support staff. They don't have to be entertained in class; they see the importance of knowledge and of taking the initiative to learn. They get involved in learning.

5. Get Guidance...

They develop their understanding of their relationship with the Holy Spirit during college; they see this relationship as central to their understanding of reality and to living out their destiny. They get guidance. They know the campus. They know the staff in their advising center, and they go there to get help with planning their goals. They know whom to talk with in the library about research. They get help from their learning center.

try A Checklist— Presentations and Papers

- On what topic does God want me to present?
- What's the purpose of my project?
- What would I like to teach my audience?
- Is my topic manageable? Is it narrow?
- Have I created a plan for researching, developing, and presenting my topic?
- What research will I use to guide me?
- Who can give me advice during the process?
- Have I created a tentative thesis statement? One that illustrates my purpose and shows my unique perspective?
- Do I have identifiable main points that support my thesis?
- What type of outline will I use? Topical? Chronological? Spatial? Have I asked my professor for a model to follow?
- Can my ideas be supported with Scripture?

Appendix
7

try A Checklist— Presenting My Ideas

- Have I asked God to guide my word choice? To help me speak with conviction? To calm my emotions? To use my presentation to help someone else?
- Who is my audience? What are their unique characteristics? Where are they in their spiritual journey?
- How can I adapt my topic to influence them most? What persuasive strategies can I use that will challenge the students and professor?
- How will I gain and maintain their attention? What quotes, stories, questions, visual aids, or statistics can I incorporate?
- Do my actions complement my words?
- Does my presentation seem like a conversation or a performance? Is it authentic?
- Have I practiced and worked beyond rough drafts?
- Have I done my best work and then moved on to other assignments?

Appendix
8

try Money Vision

Vision: Write down your vision for your money/stuff during college. Ask God to help you see your resources the way He does. If you waste what you have now, how will you know what God's best is for your future? Whom are you supposed to help with your resources?

Reality: Be practical. Take steps to make sure that your vision becomes a reality. Be faithful with what you have, and watch as God uses you to help others and provides you with a great sense of freedom. Take action by writing down your vision and the steps you'll take to see it through.

Example

Vision: I want to understand what God has to say about the money I have. I see myself living practical and using God's advice on how to make my best financial choices. I see myself saving money and being financially free during college and when I graduate. If I'm free, I won't feel pressure to pursue a career that's not for me. I share what I have with others and continue to do my best with what I have. I'm content with what God gives me. I know that everything I am and all that I have belongs to God.

Reality Steps:
- I'll keep my heart sensitive to God about money. I'll give cheerfully to Him.
- I'll make saving money a priority.
- I'll practice wisdom when spending. I'll write down Proverbs 13:11 and keep it in my wallet.
- I'll sponsor a child through WorldVision or give to an integrity-filled ministry.

- I'll get wise advice when making money/stuff decisions.
- I'll keep track of what God gives me by creating a three-part budget. I'll give to God, save some, and spend some.

try Vision to Reality

- What personal qualities will be most important for helping you reach your goals?

- What strengths have you been entrusted with that will help you be your best?

- What spiritual principles will you rely on to help you reach your goals?

- What career areas are you most interested in?

- Write out your personal mission statement for college. How can developing your ability help you fulfill your mission?

try 3 Learning Steps— Seeing to Living

1. See it: Visualize you at your best with academics. What types of things are you doing? What is your attitude like?

2. Be it: Realize where you are right now in your ability. What skills do you have? What are your weaknesses? What is your attitude like?

3. Live it: Take action to make sure that your ideal self becomes your real self. What steps can you take to ensure that the vision of you at your best becomes real? Who can help you get the skills you need to succeed in your courses?

Practice Learning (take steps)

1. See It:

- Take a moment to write down a description of you at your best in college.

_____

_____

_____

_____

_____

2. Be It:

- How committed are you to doing your best academically?
- How confident are you that you can succeed with learning?

- How do you view your performance up to now?
- Where would you like to be after this semester? When you graduate?
- In your words, what has kept you from doing your best in the past?
- Who can you talk with about improving your ability to learn?

3. Live It:

- Write down all of the learning barriers that you can think of in the right column.
- List all the strategies that you can use to overcome your barriers. Get advice about your action plan.

Take Action	Barriers
Examples: • I'll talk with my professors about course expectations and about grading policies. Ask her for tips on taking essay tests. Follow up by getting tips from the writing center. • I'll say yes to learning and no to activities that don't line up with my academic priorities. Change my perspective of time. Learn to manage my time. Talk with my academic counselor about tips. Buy a book on time management. • Ask God to give me a new perspective. • I'll learn about the benefits of college and talk with a career and academic counselor about the importance of learning new skills.	**Examples:** • I didn't know what my history teacher expected on the tests. • I had too much going on. • I don't see the point in doing well in these classes.

try Stress Management

*...give me an **undivided** heart.*

—Psalm 86:11

One: Remember that you have an audience of one; focus on the priorities He gives you. Learn to simplify your life.

No: Learn to be assertive and to say no during college. When you say no to certain people and things, you free yourself to say yes when the time is right.

Excellence: Pursue excellence instead of perfection. Focus on doing your best with the time you have been given. Live excellently, and let God see you as perfect because of His Son.

Happiness: Choose to have a positive attitude. Even the negative things that happen to us are used for good.

Eat Right: The right foods will help you make your best decisions (Isaiah 7:15).

Accept Responsibility: Keep yourself focused on getting your assignments done ahead of time. Prepare rather than procrastinate.

Refuge: Find a quiet, relaxing place to go on campus. Go there several times during the week. Read through the Psalms during the semester, and take refuge in the promise of His comfort this very moment. Tell Him about your week, and listen to what He wants to tell you.

Talk: Share and carry stress with others; talk with friends with perspective about your experiences and how best to handle stress. Good relationship, with lots of laughing, is the best remedy for stress. Remember, it's the small things that take away from the quality of your college experience. Choose to maintain an undivided heart and a focused life.

try **Relationship Peace**

DID YOU KNOW THAT many college campuses have an office devoted entirely to helping resolve campus conflict? Think about it. With all of the personalities and perspectives on campus, why wouldn't you need an office to help manage the potential disagreements? These offices generally offer tips for handling any type of conflict that might occur on a campus, conflict you might have with your roommate, another student, or with a professor or staff member.

Conflict, if handled effectively, can help you strengthen your relationships. It can keep issues from festering and growing to unnecessary levels. If handled incorrectly, conflict can have devastating consequences. When Daniel was faced with potential conflict, he handled it with "wisdom and tact" (Daniel 2:14). The king was furious because no one was able to interpret his dream, so he ordered that all the wise men in Babylon, which included Daniel and his friends, be killed. Daniel defused the situation by first using a question, and then he followed by asking for time to interpret the dream. Once he received permission to interpret the dream, he returned to his friends and asked that they pray to God for mercy. Because Daniel handled conflict correctly, he saved the lives of many, including his own.

Get help with conflict during college. Talk with a trained counselor on campus or go to your campus mediation office. Be like Daniel; learn to keep calm during turbulent times. Act with wisdom, use effective questions, continue by asking for some time to think about the issue, and stay in prayer. Finish by taking the right action to make sure the conflict is resolved.

try Higher Transitions

transition: *"an act, process, or instance of changing from one state, form, activity, or place to another"*[1]

DURING COLLEGE, I HEARD a pastor compare our transitions in life to a flying trapeze act. College is definitely like that. As a student, you have to let go of one trapeze bar, fly midair for what often feels never-ending, and then successfully grab the next trapeze bar as it comes your way.

When you transition from high school to college, you have to let go, soar into the unknown, and successfully find your grip on your freshman year. Each year of college works like this. If you transferred from a community college to a four-year school, then you know this feeling of mid-air exhilaration and apprehension that's often referred to as transfer shock. If you are getting ready to transition into graduate or professional school or into a job, then you will soon know the flying trapeze feeling.

How you view transitions and how you handle them during college is exceedingly important. Humbling ourselves before God allows our inner person to hear His voice. We comprehend His deep purpose for these changes. He's not just moving us to a different school or into a different environment; He's changing our internal landscape. He's growing us up, shaping us into His vision for us, so that we can be the person He can use.

If you live in a listening state you will know when to let go of one bar and reach for what God has next. God is very much concerned about timing in your life. Don't force anything as you're waiting to see which direction to go next. He delays for our good so our trust can grow.

Work hard at planting seeds, but don't try to force them to grow. If you're graduating and waiting on your next opportunity, humble yourself and remember that His purpose and timing are perfect.

try Spiritual Preparation—
Five Tips

I TALKED WITH A STUDENT who had gone to great length to prepare academically for college. He had taken AP courses and had done well on the entrance exam. He had prepared, like many students, in every way that he thought he could for college.

I had talked with him after he had failed several courses during his first year. When I asked him what went wrong, he commented, "I thought I already knew most of what I was taking, so I blew off those courses." He was quick to admit that his academic arrogance, his attitude of knowing everything, had kept him from making academic progress his freshman year.

If he'd prepared his heart for college, he would've saved himself the trouble of retaking courses and wasting his money. Preparing your heart will help you academically and in every other area during college.

1. Ask God to give you a heart that's sensitive to His leading during college. This is your preeminent guard for being your best.
2. Ask God to help you and look for His hand in the details of your life. This perspective will help you make the most of every opportunity. You'll do what it takes to make small, steady steps in learning. You'll live each day with direction.
3. Pray and discuss with your parents, friends, mentors, and teachers what your purpose during college is. Start by discussing your opportunity for serving God during college. Follow with conversation about your interest, what you like to study, and the areas they see as your strengths and weaknesses.

4. Get advice. Meet with a guidance counselor to see which school might best meet your needs. Be practical here. Think about where you currently are academically, how much you would like to pay, and which temptations you would like to avoid. I talked with an optometrist once who said he started off at a smaller state school because he didn't want to get caught up in the party scene for which his state's large university was known. His forward thinking and knowledge of his weaknesses paid off.
5. Build up your immunity to empty teaching by learning for yourself what the Christian faith is all about. Once you've done this, become familiar with worldviews (this is not for the immature or young Christian!). Talk with your family or ask your youth minister to do a study on world religions and worldviews. If handled right, this can immunize your belief system; it's like a vaccination shot for your faith.

try College Resources

AS YOU CONTINUE WITH college, remember to make your plans by seeking advice. Your best decisions will require research and wise counsel. You can start by using the resources that your campus provides. Talk with your advisors and ask them to suggest helpful resources. Here are some starting points. Many of these organizations have helpful on-line publications and newsletters, so you might look into subscribing.

Spiritual Guidance and Reality

Get involved with a Bible-based, local church. Here are a several spiritual resources you can check out. Use these resources to stay connected to truth during college. If these ministries offer newsletters, I suggest you sign up to receive them.

BreakPoint: breakpoint.org
Campus Crusade for Christ International: ccci.org/
Fixed-Point Foundation: fixed-point.org
Josh McDowell Ministry: www.josh.org
Lee Strobel: leestrobel.com
Ravi Zacharias International Ministries: rzim.org
Trevor's website: tryhigher.com

Relationships

Stay connected to the right people during college. Check out these resources to help you live out your best relationships.

Drs. Les and Leslie Parrott: realrelationships.com
Cloud-Townsend Solutions for Life: cloudtownsend.com

Your Leadership Skills

Take advantage of the many leadership programs on your campus. Also, check into internship or leadership experiences at your church or favorite ministry. Use the summer to work as a camp counselor, or see the value in doing your best with your summer job. Here are a couple of programs that many campuses support. For example, the Emerging Leaders program is "a highly competitive program that places college students with disabilities in fulfilling summer internships and provides them with leadership development opportunities. Emerging leaders partners with businesses to help them find outstanding young talent while also considering diversity and inclusion in their hiring practices."

Emerging Leaders: emerging-leaders.com
John Maxwell: Injoy.com
LeaderShape: www.leadershape.com

Health and Wellness

Take charge of your physical and mental health during college. Use some of these resources to get you started.

Dr. Colbert: drcolbert.com
Meier Clinics: meierclinics.com
New Life Ministries: newlife.com
Rubin Jordan: makersdiet.com

Study Abroad

If you get the chance and you have the money for it, consider studying abroad during college. There are summer, semester, and year-long programs. Many schools offer some great scholarships to help you pay for these learning trips. If you're mature, have a good support group to go with, and you're ready for an adventure, then this can be a great way to broaden your vision! If you can't afford it and the scholarship thing doesn't work out, don't stress out about missing the chance. Just set your sights on traveling during graduate school or when you're finished with school and you've saved up for it. You're a learner for life, so traveling is something that can be a part of your future.

Food for the Hungry: go-ed.net
GoAbroad.com: goabroad.com
Institute of International Education: iie.org
Study Abroad: studyabroad.com
U.S. Department of State Bureau of Educational and Cultural Affairs: www.exchanges.state.gov

Attending College

American Council on Education and Lumina Foundation: knowhow2go.org/
CollegeBoard: collegeboard.com
Pathways to College Network: www.pathwaystocollege.net
Success4Students: www.success4students.com

Jobs and Majors

There are lots of great ways to explore your major and career interests. Start by talking with your academic and career counselors. Find out what your school offers. Take a career exploration course. Your career counselor can show you how to bridge the gap between your major and a job.

Here are some things your career counselor can offer:

- Personality Assessments
- Career Coaching
- Resume Tips
- Job Search Strategies and Resources

- Interviewing Tips
- Graduate School Preparation

The U.S. Department of Labor updates this helpful handbook every year.

Occupational Outlook Handbook (OOH): bls.gov/OCO/

Money During College

Do your homework when making choices about money during college. To live in freedom, use biblical principles when making money choices. Use some of these resources to help you create a guide to managing your resources.

Crown Financial Ministries: crown.org
Dave Ramsey: daveramsey.com
Federal Student Aid: federalstudentaid.ed.gov
The College Trap: www.thecollegetrap.com

Endnotes

Introduction

1. G.K. Chesterton, http://www.worldofquotes.com/author/G.-K.-Chesterton/1/index.html (accessed February 27th, 2009).
2. Psalm 61:2.

Chapter 2—A Higher Education

1. C.G. Jung, "The Development of Personality" *The Self.* (Clark Moustakas. Merril-Palmer School, Detroit: Harper and Row, New York and Evanston, 1956): 157.

Chapter 3—Purpose during College

1. Christopher J. Lucas, *American Higher Education: A History* (New York: St. Martin's Griffin, 1996), 69.
2. Rich Stearns, "Alma Mater," *WorldVision* (Autumn 2007): 4.
3. Ibid.

Chapter 5—Small Things, Big Heart

1. Mother Teresa, http://www.brainyquote.com/quotes/quotes/m/mothertere153715.html (accessed June 14th, 2009).

Chapter 6—Just Shine

1. Charles Swindoll as quoted in Bob Kelly, *Worth Repeating: More than 5,000 Classic and Contemporary Quotes* (Grand Rapids Michigan: Kregel Publications), 312.
2. Josh McDowell, *More Than a Carpenter* (Wheaton Illinois: Living Books, Tyndale Publishers, 1977), 119-120.
3. Josh McDowell, Evidence that Demands a Verdict (San Bernardino, CA. Campus Crusade, 1972).
4. Statistics on college students, http://nces.ed.gov/pubsearch/pubsinfo.asp?pubid=2006184.
5. Charles Malik as quoted in C.S. Lewis Foundation, http://www.cslewis.org/about/ourmission.html (accessed June 27, 2008).

6. J Stanley Mattson as quoted in the C.S. Lewis Foundation, http://www. cslewis.org/about/ourmission.html (accessed June 27, 2008).

7. Mohandas Gandhi as quoted on, http://www.brainyquote.com/quotes/ quotes/m/mohandasga130962.html (accessed February 23, 2008).

Chapter 7—About Truth

8. Charles Colson, *How Now Shall We Live?* (Wheaton, Illinois: Tyndale House Publishers, 1999), 34.

9. John R. Thelin, *A History of American Higher Education* (Baltimore, Maryland: The Johns Hopkins University Press, 2004), 41.

10. Dietrich Bonhoeffer, *Ethics* (New York: Simon and Schuster Inc, 1995), 70.

11. John R. Thelin, *A History of American Higher Education* (Baltimore, Maryland: The Johns Hopkins University Press, 2004), 41.

12. John Bunyan, *The Pilgrim's Progress* (London, England: Penguin Books, 1987), 28-29.

13. Ephesians 4:15.

14. C.S. Lewis as quoted in Wayne Martindale and Jerry Root (Eds), *The Quotable Lewis* (Wheaton Illinois: Tyndale House Publishers, 1989) 473.

Chapter 8—A Compelling Choice

1. Mark A. Beliles and Stephen K. McDowell, *America's Providential History* (Charlottesville, Virginia: Providence Foundation, 1991), 109.

2. Patricia Amason (Ed), *Fundamentals of Communication* (2nd Edition) (Boston MA: Pearson Custom Publishing, 2006), 32.

3. 1 John 2:16.

4. Stephen R. Covey, A. Roger Merrill, and Rebecca R. Merrill, *First Things First* (New York, NY: Fireside), 59.

5. The illustration given is my own adaption of Perry's Model of student development. For a detailed discussion of Perry's model, see William Perry as quoted in Nancy J. Evans, Deanna S. Forney, Florence Guido-Dibrito. *Student Development in College: Theory, Research, and Practice* (San Francisco, CA: Jossey-Bass, 1998), 131.

6. R. Coles, *The Moral Life of Children* (Boston, MA: Atlantic Monthly Press, 1986), 21.

7. C.S. Lewis as quoted in Wayne Martindale and Jerry Root (Eds), *The Quotable Lewis* (Wheaton Illionoise: Tyndale House Publishers, 1989) 340.

8. Psalm 61:2.

9. Oswald Chambers, *My Utmost for His Highest* edited by James Reiman (Grand Rapids MI: Discovery House Publishers, 1992) July 27th.

Chapter 9—Spirit-Filled Learning

1. Mark Twain, http://thinkexist.com/quotation/i-never-let-schooling-interfere-with-my-education/1211759.html (accessed June 14th, 2009).

2. Benjamin S. Bloom, as quoted in David R. Krathwohl, "A Revision of Bloom's Taxonomy: An Overview," *Theory Into Practice* 41, no 8. (Autumn 2002): 215.

3. Herman Helmholtz as quoted in Ben Carson, *Think Big* (Grand Rapids, Michigan: Zondervan Publishing House, 1992), 183.

Chapter 10—Motivation

1. L. Braskamp and M. Maehr, *The Motivation Factor: A Theory of Personal Investment.* (Lexington: D.C. Heath and Company, 1986).

2. Thomas Kelly as quoted in Charles Swindoll, *The Tale of the Tardy Oxcart: And 1,501 Other Stories* (Nashville TN: Word Publishing, 1998) 212.

3. John Bunyan, *The Pilgrim's Progress* (London: Penguin Books, 1987), 28-29.

4. Alex Harris and Brett Harris, *Do Hard Things* (Colorado Springs, CO: Multnomah Books, 2008), 212-213.

5. Mark Victor Hansen and Joe Batten, *The Master Motivator.* (New York: Barnes and Noble Publishing, 2005).

Chapter 11—Go to the Ant

1. Miles J. Stanford as quoted in Charles Swindoll, *The Tale of the Tardy Oxcart: And 1,501 Other Stories* (Nashville TN: Word Publishing, 1998), 173.

Chapter 12—Communicate

1. Trevor Francis and Michael T. Miller, "Communication Apprehension: Levels of First-Generation College Students at 2-Year Institutions," *Community College Journal of Research and Practice*, 32 (2008): 45.

2. Proverbs 16:23 (NASB).

3. Braveheart, http://www.imdb.com/title/tt0112573/quotes (accessed February 26th, 2009).

4. W. Dauphinais, "Forging the Path to Power," *Security Management* (1997, 41, 21-23.

5. Billy Graham, *Just as I Am* (San Francisco: Zondervan, 1997) 49.

6. Ibid.

7. Unpublished qualitative data from Trevor Francis, "A Comparison of The Self-Reported Levels of Oral Communication Apprehension" (Fayetteville Arkansas: University of Arkansas, 2007).

8. See James C. McCroskey's chapter "Willingness to Communicate, Communication Apprehension, and Self-Perceived Communication Competence: Conceptualizations and Perspectives" in *Avoiding Communication: Shyness, Reticence, and Communication Apprehension* (Cresskill, New Jersey: Hampton Press, 1997) for an in-depth explanation of his concept of Communication Apprehension (CA).

9. Patricia Amason (Ed), *Fundamentals of Communication* (2nd Edition) (Boston MA: Pearson Custom Publishing, 2006), 100.

10. Michael J. Papa, & Ethel C. Glenn, "Listening Ability and Performance with New Technology: A Case Study," *The Journal of Business Communication* (1988), 25, 5-16.

11. D.B. Curtis, J.L. Winsor, and R.D. Stephens, "National Preferences in Business and Communication Education," Communication Education (1989) 38, 6-14.

12. The Cornell Note-Taking System, http://ccc.byu.edu/learning/ note-tak.php (accessed on January 23rd, 2009).

Chapter 13—Relentless Relationships

1. Sir Roger Bannister, http://www.achievement.org/autodoc/page/ ban0bio-1 (accessed January 23rd, 2009).

2. George Ritzer, *McDonaldization: The Reader*. (Thousand Oaks, California: Pine Forge Press, 2002), 20.

3. Richard Light, "*Making the Most of College,*" Cambridge, MA. Harvard University Press (2004). p. 81.

4. Ravi Zacharias, *I Isaac, Take Thee, Rebeka: Moving from Romance to Lasting Love* (Nashville, Tennessee: Word Publishing, 2004).

5. Les Parrot and Leslie Parrot, *Relationships (*Grand Rapids, MI: Zondervan Publishing, 1998), 20.

6. Eric Ludy and Leslie Ludy, *When Dreams Come True* (Sisters, OR: Loyal Publishing, 2000), 251.

7. Richard Land, http://insight.faithandfamily.com/archive/topic/singles/ (accessed July 5th, 2008).

8. Read C.S. Lewis's Mere Christianity.

Chapter 14—Isolated or Inspired?

1. Ron Hall and Denver Moore, with Lynn Vincent, *Same Kind of Different as Me* (Thomas Nelson), 235.

2. Florida Community College, http://www.fccj.org/friends/index.html (accessed on September 4th, 2008).

3. College Board, http://www.collegeboard.com/student/csearch/where-to-start/150494.html (accessed September 4th, 2008).

4. Rudy, http://www.rudyinternational.com/ (accessed February 26th, 2009).

5. See Anthony R. D'Augelli, Arnold H. Grossman, Nicholas P. Salter, Joseph J Vasey, Michael T. Starks, Katerina O. Sinclair. "Predicting the Suicide Attempts of Lesbian, Gay, and Bisexual Youth," *Suicide and Life-Threatening Behavior* 35, no. 6 (December 2005). See also Arnold H. Grossman, Anthony R. D'Augelli "Transgender Youth and Life-Threatening Behaviors," *Suicide and Life-Threatening Behavior* 37, no. 5 (October 2007).

6. See www.NARTH.com.

7. Chad W. Thompson, *Loving Homosexuals as Jesus Would: A Fresh Christian Approach* (Grand Rapids, MI: BrazosPress, 2004).

8. See www.Exodus.com.

9. Lawrence M. Rudner, as quoted in Chuck Colson and Nancy Pearcey, How Now Shall We Live? (Wheaton, Illinois: Tyndale, 1999),524.

10. Linda Montgomery's research as quoted in Brian D. Ray, "Homeschoolers on to College: What Research Shows Us," *Journal of College Admissions*: 3. Brian D. Ray, "Homeschoolers on to College: What Research Shows Us," *Journal of College Admission*. FindArticles.com. 25 Apr, 2009. http://findarticles.com/p/articles/mi_qa3955/is_200410/ai_n9443747/.

11. Chuck Colson and Nancy Pearcey, How Now Shall We Live? (Wheaton, Illinois: Tyndale, 1999), 339.

12. Brian D. Ray, "Homeschoolers on to College: What Research Shows Us," *Journal of College Admissions*: 5.

13. Psalm 131:1-2.

14. S.P. Choy, "Nontraditional Undergraduates: Findings from the Condition of Education," (2002), National Center for Education, http://nces.ed.gov/pubs2002/2002012.pdf (accessed April 12, 2006).

15. Laura Rendon, http://www.eric.ed.gov/ERICDocs/data/ericdocs2sql/content_storage_01/0000019b/80/29/ac/58.pdf (accessed June 14th, 2009).

16. E. Broughton and M. Neyer, "Advising and Counseling Student Athletes," *New Direction for Student Services* (2001): 47.

17. See J.J. Valentine and D. J. Taub, "Responding to the Developmental Needs of Student Athletes," Journal of College Counseling (1999).

18. See Brandon Burlsworth Foundation, brandonburlsworth.org. See also http://en.wikipedia.org/wiki/Brandon_Burlsworth (accessed July 28th, 2008).

19. Chariots of Fire http://www.imdb.com/title/tt0082158/quotes (accessed February 25th, 2009).

20. brandonburlsworth.org or read Jeff Kinley's *Through the Eyes of a Champion.*

21. Lyle A. Gohn and Ginger R. Albin (Eds), *Understanding College Student Subpopulations: A Guide for Student Affairs Professionals* (National Association of Student Personnel Administrators, 2006), 135.

22. John Maxwell, *Developing the Leader Within You* (Nashville, TN: Thomas Nelson Publishers, 1993), 80.

23. LifeWithoutLimbs, Nick Vujicic, http://www.youtube.com/ watch?v=TtweZxNGk1Y (accessed July 28th, 2008).

24. See www.giannajessen.com.

25. Laura I. Rendon, Romero E. Jalomo, and Amaury Nora, "Theoretical Considerations in the Study of Minority Student Retention in Higher Education" in Frances K. Stage, Deborah Faye Carter, Don Hossler, and Edward P. St. John, *Theoretical Perspectives on College Students*, eds. (Boston, MA: Pearson Custom Publishing, 2003), 519.

26. Mary E. Levin and Joel R. Levin, "A Critical Examination of Academic Retention Programs for At-Risk Minority College Students," *Journal of College Student Development* (1991), volume 32, p. 324.

27. Anson and Marchesani as quoted in Edward G. Whipple and Eileen G. Sullivan "Greek Letter Organizations: Communinities of Learners?," *New Directions for Student Services*, no. 81 (1998): 15.

28. J. L. Baier and E.G. Whipple as quoted in Edward G. Whipple and Eileen G. Sullivan "Greek Letter Organizations: Communinities of Learners?," *New Directions for Student Services*, no. 81 (1998): 15.

29. See Ernest T. Pascarella, Lamont Flowers, and Elizabeth J. Whitt, "Cognitive Effects of Greek Affliation in College: Additional Evidence," *NASPA Journal*, 38, no. 3 (Spring 2007). Negative cognitive effects of Greek Affiliation were occurred primarily in the first year of college. See also Suzanne M. Kilgannon and T. Dary Erwin, "A Longitudinal Study about the Identity and Moral Development of Greek Students," *Journal of College Student Development*, 33, no. 3 (1992): 253-259.

30. T. Tuttle, J. McKinney, and M. Rago, "College Students Working: The Choice Nexus," Indiana Project on Academic Success (2005), http://www. indiana.edu/~ipas1/workingstudentbrief.pdf (accessed April 12th, 2006).

31. L. Horn and S. Nevill, "Profile of Undergraduates in U.S. Postsecondary Education Institutions: 2003-04: With a Special Analysis of Community College Students" National Center for Education Statistics (2006) http://www.nces.ed.gov/pubsearch/pubsinfo. asp?pubid=2006184(accessed April 24, 2009).

32. Stephen R. Covey, A. Roger Merrill, and Rebecca R. Merrill, *First Things First* (New York, NY: Fireside), 59.

Chapter 15—Confident Students

1. Martin E. P. Seligman, *Learned Optimism* (New York: Alfred A. Knopf, Inc., 1990), 153.

2. Anthony Campolo as quoted in Charles Swindoll, *The Tale of the Tardy Oxcart: And 1,501 Other Stories* (Nashville TN: Word Publishing, 1998), 302-303.

3. For a detailed description of this research, see Martin E. P. Seligman, *Learned Optimism* (New York: Alfred A. Knopf, Inc., 1990).

4. Joyce Meyer.

Chapter 16—Vivid Perspective

1. J. William Fulbright quoted in Catalog of Studies, University of Arkansas, (2008-2009), 114.

2. Oswald Chambers, *My Utmost for His Highest* (Uhrichsville, OH: Barbour Publishing, 1963), May 9th.

3. Research quoted in Alina Tugend, "The Many Errors in Thinking About Mistakes," *The New York Times* (November 24, 2007).

4. Lori Holyfield, *Moving Up and Out: Poverty, Education, and the Single Parent Family*. Philadelphia, PA: Temple University Press, 2002).

5. Warren Webster as quoted in Charles Swindoll, *The Tale of the Tardy Oxcart: And 1,501 Other Stories* (Nashville TN: Word Publishing, 1998), 300.

Chapter 17—Four Significant Years

1. Frank Minirth, *Brilliant Mind: Proven Ways to Increase Your Brainpower* (Grand Rapids, MI: Revel, 2007).

2. Dr. Colbert's book *The Bible Cure for Stress* (Lake Mary, FL. Strang Communication, 2002).

3. Herant A. Katchadourian and John Boli, *Careerism and Intellectualism Among College Students* (San Francisco, CA: Jossey-Bass Inc. Publishers, 1985), 58.

4. Jordan S. Rubin, *The Maker's Diet: The 40-Day Health Experience That Will Change Your Life Forever* (Lake Mary, FL: Siloam, 2005).

5. Ibid., 65.

Chapter 18—Your Purpose, God's Provision

1. Os Guiness, *The Call: Finding and Fulfilling the Central Purpose of Life* (Nashville: Word, 1998), 73.

2. Nick Vujicic, Life Without Limbs, LifeWithoutLimbs.org, Newsletter (August 2008).

3. Dave Ramsey, *Money Matters: Quick Answers to Your Everyday Financial Questions* (New York, NY: MIF Books, 2004), 111.

Chapter 19—Discover Your Destiny during College

1. My descriptions and illustrations were based on Chickering's "Seven Vectors." For a detailed discussion of Chickering's work, see Nancy J. Evans, Deanna S. Forney, Florence Guido-Dibrito. *Student Development in College: Theory, Research, and Practice* (San Francisco, CA: Jossey-Bass, 1998), 38-40.

2. Donald Asher, *How to Get Any Job with Any Major* (Berkeley CA: Ten Speed Press, 2004), 11-12. .

3. Frank Minirth and Paul Meier, *Happiness is a Choice* (Grand Rapids, MI: Revell, 1994).

4. Don Colbert, *Deadly Emotions: Understanding the Mind-Body-Spirit Connection that Can Heal or Destroy You* (Nashville, TN: Thomas Nelson Publishers, 2003).

5. Adrian Rogers, *What Every Christian Ought to Know* (Nashville, TN: Broadman and Holman Publishers, 2005), 111.

6. Alexander Astin, *What Matters in College? Four Critical Years Revisited* (San Francisco, CA: Jossey-Bass, 1993), 398.

7. Henry Cloud, John Townsend,*Boundaries (When to say YES When to Say No To Take Control of Your Life)* (Grand Rapids, MI: Zondervan. 2001).

8. Les and Leslie Parrott, *Relationships* (Grand Rapids, MI: Zondervan 2002).

9. Arthur Miller Jr., *Why You Can't Be Anything You Want to Be* (Grand Rapids, MI: Zondervan Publishers, 1999), 98.

10. Richard Bolles, *How to Find Your Mission in Life* (Berkeley, CA: Ten Speed Press, 2000), 49.

11. Oswald Chambers.

12. Herbert P. Hess as quoted in C. William Pollard, *Serving Two Masters: Reflections on God and Profit* (New York, NY: HarperCollins Publishers), xvi.

13. Herbert Spencer as quoted in Charles Swindoll, *The Tale of the Tardy Oxcart: And 1,501 Other Stories* (Nashville TN: Word Publishing, 1998), 66.

14. Tom Petty, http://www.quotesdaddy.com/author/Tom+Petty (accessed February 16th, 2009).

15. Oswald Chambers, *My Utmost for His Highest* (Uhrichsville, OH: Barbour Publishing, 1963), November 2nd.

Appendix 3— *try* A College Plan

1. James Dobson, *Life on the Edge: A Young Adults Life to a Meaningful Future* (Dallas, Texas: Word, 1995), 3.

Appendix 4— *try* Focused Motivation!

1. My ideas for this student exercise were based on James O. Hammons "Task Analysis" (Fayetteville, AR: Higher Education Leadership Program, University of Arkansas, 1999).

Appendix 13— *try* Higher Transitions

1. Webster's II New College Dictionary (Boston, MA: Houghton Mifflin Company, 2001).

About the Author

TREVOR FRANCIS, ED.D., IS an award-winning academic counselor, speaker, and founder of Higher International, a ministry
promoting spiritual leadership on college campuses. Trevor is
a graduate of the University of Arkansas's Higher Education
Leadership Program. He enjoys learning, discussing true spirituality, and being with Nicole, his wife and best friend. You can visit
their website at **tryhigher.com**.